J. WAYNE FEARS

THE COMPLETE BOOK OF
DUTCH OVEN COOKING

SKYHORSE PUBLISHING

Skyhorse Publishing books may be purchased in bulk at special discounts for sales promotion, corporate gifts, fund-raising, or educational purposes. Special editions can also be created to specifications. For details, contact the Special Sales Department, Skyhorse Publishing, 555 Eighth Avenue, Suite 903, New York, NY 10018 or info@skyhorsepublishing.com.

www.skyhorsepublishing.com

10 9 8 7 6 5 4 3 2 1

Library of Congress Cataloging-in-Publication Data is available on file.
ISBN: 978-1-60239-963-1

Printed in the United States of America

PHOTOGRAPHY CREDITS:
Barry Fikes: *Cover photo*
Vann Cleveland; *6, 72, 86, 138*
Barry Fikes; *20, 22, 32, 33, 35(top), 50,*
51, 52, 53, 54, 55, 56(top), 58, 76, 87
Alex Bowers; *95, 96, 99, 100, 104, 107,*
108, 111, 112, 115, 116, 119, 120, 125,
126, 129, 133, 134, 137

CONTENTS

To Sofee
She brings sunshine to every day, every situation.

INTRODUCTION

I f you saw a TV commercial that advertised one cooking pot that would bake bread, steam vegetables, boil shrimp, fry eggs, stew wild game, and broil meats, chances are you might be interested. But what if the commercial went on to say that this non-stick pot could be used to cook a meal on your home stove, in your den fireplace, on the patio, in a campfire at a state park, or on family camping trips, plus it was guaranteed to last several generations of use? Your interest would probably peak and you would want to know a lot more about this magic pot.

The magic cook pot that can do it all is the Dutch oven.

THIS MAGIC POT IS THE DUTCH OVEN

There are a lot of different designs of cooking pots that are called "Dutch ovens." Some are modern aluminum pots designed to be used with modern stoves. Others are cast iron pots with legs that have been made famous by cooks on African safaris. (The real name for these pots is *potjie* and it dates back to the 1500s.) Yet others are cast iron pots with rounded bottoms that are designed to be used hanging over an open fire. And there are flat-bottomed cast iron pots designed to sit on a stove. These are often called kitchen Dutch ovens. I have used them all with satisfaction, while debating against their being called Dutch ovens.

Most outdoor cooks are in agreement that the real Dutch oven is made from heavy cast iron, or aluminum, with a flat bottom sitting on three short legs protruding about two inches. It has a strong wire bail. The lid is made of the same heavy cast iron and has a small loop handle in the center. The rim of the lid is flanged so that hot coals will stay on the lid while cooking. Many people call these ovens "camp Dutch ovens" to distinguish them from other so-called Dutch ovens. For the purpose of this book this is the Dutch oven we will be talking about.

J. Wayne Fears has counted on the Dutch oven to produce good meals throughout his outdoor career. It has never let him down.

The Dutch oven has been piquing cooks' interest for many centuries. It has been used in this country since the first settlers began exploring the Atlantic seaboard. Today, 21st-century cooks are finding the "old-fashioned" Dutch oven just as much fun and valuable as did the colonial cooks who depended upon the pots to cook all their meals. While we don't have to stoop over a fireplace full of hot coals to cook a meal, cooks around the world are discovering the joy and good taste that come with cooking in a Dutch oven. Whether they are used for cooking for a party on the patio, cooking on a camping trip, or cooking in an emergency when the utilities are not working, the Dutch oven produces great-tasting food with a small amount of effort, and its use is a fun family activity.

MY LIFE WITH DUTCH OVENS

My earliest recollection of the Dutch oven was as a small child growing up in the mountains of Alabama. My dad was a trapper and, occasionally, would take me on his trapping expeditions. He had the simplest of camping gear but his camps were comfortable and the meals always good and plentiful. His cook kit was an old 10-inch cast iron Dutch oven. The night before we would leave to run his traps, I would lie awake in my bed too excited to sleep. I would visualize the old Dutch oven steaming on the campfire, full of stew. I could smell the hoe-cake he would be cooking on the inverted oven lid sitting on a small bed of coals. Morning would not come quick enough. He was a master at cooking in the black pot and today, more than 50 years later, I use the same Dutch oven to cook for friends and family on my patio. Every time I cook in the pot I think about those long-ago adventures with my dad, and the many meals we shared that were prepared in his Dutch oven.

At the age of eleven I joined the Boy Scouts and was surprised that Dutch oven cooking was a part of the skill training required if you were to be an active member of Troop 70. By the time I earned the rank of Eagle, I could cook up a pretty fair meal for a patrol-size group of scouts using a couple of Dutch ovens. It was during this period I was introduced to aluminum Dutch ovens and learned how to use them in conjunction with the cast iron ovens.

As I reached adulthood I was to find the Dutch oven to continue to be a part of my life. The cooking skills I learned in Troop 70 would come in handy countless times in the future. A career that combined wildlife management with outdoor writing found me working in remote camps throughout the world. From the frozen Arctic to southern Argentina I would work out of camps that depended on the Dutch oven to provide hungry outdoorsmen with good-tasting, wholesome meals. For several years I worked as an outfitter and guide with backcountry operations in Alaska, British Columbia, Colorado, Georgia, and Alabama. To feed my guests, I depended upon various sizes of cast iron Dutch ovens and was a constant student of Dutch oven cooking.

DUTCH OVENS AT HOME

During the off-seasons I would bring my Dutch ovens home and store them by the fireplace in the family room of my home. Here they became the center of attention as visitors would ask about the "antiques" and whether I really used them. This gave me the idea to use the ovens to cook meals for dinner parties. Sometimes I would cook in the fireplace, as did our forefathers; on other occasions I would use charcoal briquets and cook out on the patio. These cooking sessions were always the highlight of the party and led to many of my friends becoming Dutch oven chefs. Also, it led to many Dutch ovens being sold for interior decoration rather than cooking purposes.

Today, Dutch oven cooking has become a favorite pastime for thousands of people from all walks of life. The Internet offers lots of Dutch oven cooking advice and recipes, some good, some bad. Dutch oven cook-offs have become popular gatherings for Dutch oven fans and tourists alike. Dutch oven enthusiasts have formed their own organization, the International Dutch Oven Society, to be a clearinghouse for Dutch oven information and to foster interest in Dutch oven cooking. For many people, Dutch oven cooking has become part of their recreational pursuit, for others—guides, cowboys, outfitters, back-to-the-landers, and people living in remote places—it is simply the way they cook hearty, wholesome meals daily.

DUTCH OVENS IN PRINT

Numerous writers have sung the praises of the Dutch oven. In 1906 famed outdoor writer Horace Kephart wrote in his best-selling book, *Book of Camping and Woodcraft,* "If it were not for its weight, [the Dutch oven] would be the best oven for outdoor use since it not only bakes buts cooks the meat and pone in its own steam." The late and great camping writer John Jobson, wrote in *Sports Afield* magazine, "The Dutch oven is undoubtedly the most amazing, versatile, useful instrument ever conceived for tasty camp cooking." New Orleans chef and cooking writer George Prechter has written, "If I were to have to choose only one vessel in which to cook, indoors or out, it would be the Dutch oven." Ted Trueblood, one of America's best-known outdoor writers in the 1960s and 70s wrote in *Field & Stream* magazine, "The Dutch oven is the greatest piece of outdoor cooking equipment I have ever used." Well-known cooking author Sylvia Bashline once wrote, "The Dutch oven is the most versatile cooking utensil ever invented."

Cow-camp cooks, hunting guides and many others use a Dutch oven as a part of their daily routine.

DON'T BE INTIMIDATED BY THE LEARNING PROCESS

As you read this book Dutch oven cooking may, at times, sound like a lot of work and take a lot of time to master. That is not the case, and I would never want anyone not to give it a try because of this. Yes, it does take a little experience to learn to care for and successfully cook with Dutch ovens, but once you get it down, it can be one of the most fun cooking experiences you can have. In fact, it is the taking care of and the ever-expanding learning process that most Dutch oven cooks find most interesting. Spend time around a group of seasoned Dutch oven cooks and you will hear a lot of conversation about seasoning techniques, the best coals to use, cooking in the wind, and always, great new recipes. So don't let the learning process scare you away from what may be a lifetime of fun and exciting eating. For many it is a hobby, and for a few it almost becomes a lifestyle.

THIS BOOK IS FOR YOU

Whether you are a beginning Dutch oven cook, a seasoned pro, or just someone who is interested in a cooking pot that has seen a lot of history, this book was written for you. I have tried to put it in a logical sequence, giving you everything you want to know about the magic pot and how to use it to prepare some of the greatest meals you will ever eat. It is not intended to be a recipe book as there are dozens of Dutch oven recipe books available and thousands of recipes available on line. I do give some recipes in the later chapters just to illustrate the variety of cooking that can be done in these ingenious ovens.

Now sit back and relax as we discuss Dutch oven know-how.

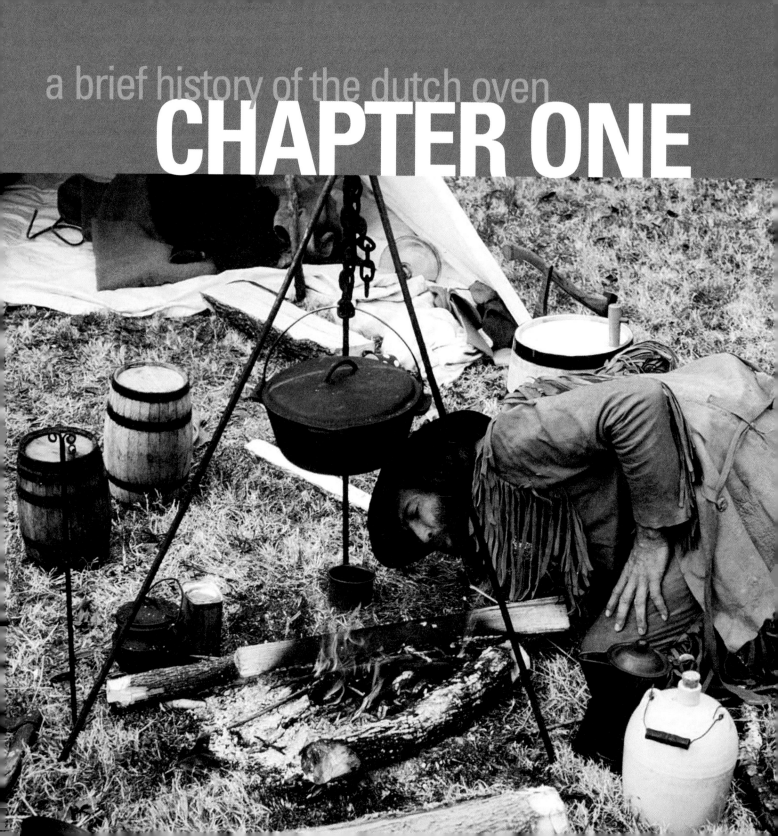

CHAPTER ONE

One of the most often-stated reasons Dutch oven cooking enthusiasts give for using the vessel is that it puts them in touch with the past; it has a touch of history associated with it. I have to agree for as I cook in my Dutch ovens I am reminded of the explorers, settlers, long-hunters, mountainmen, and cowboys who mastered the oven long before I came along.

EARLY HISTORY OF CAST IRON COOKING POTS

Researching the history of the Dutch oven was not as easy as I had anticipated, for much of it dates back to times when little written history survived about cook pots. The earliest mention I can find is a reference about cast iron cooking vessels is the seventh century. Later, during the reign of Edward III, in the 1300s, iron cooking pots and skillets were considered part of the "Crown Jewels."

While we don't know for sure that Columbus used cast iron cooking pots on his trips to the "New World," we do know that ships at that time, and later, used iron kettles in which to cook meals. They had sandboxes where the cook built a fire and, during calm seas, meals were cooked in the kettles hung over the fires. There is some reference to the Pilgrims cooking in such a fashion when they came across the Atlantic to the New World. We do know that cast iron pots, usually referred to as kettles or cooking kettles, were made in America as early as 1650. Cast aluminum Dutch ovens didn't appear until about 1889.

The Dutch ovens we use today evolved from cast iron cookware depended upon by early Americans.

THE EMERGENCE OF THE DUTCH OVEN WE KNOW TODAY

Dutch ovens as we know them today were developed in the early 18th century. The use of heavy cast iron cookware was highly regarded in Europe, as heat was evenly distributed through the pot, and there was a rapidly growing demand for cast iron cooking pots in America. The iron stove had not been invented and most cooking was done on hearths of fireplaces, outdoors over campfires, or over open fires in a lean-to behind a home. A cast iron pot was emerging that was ideal for this type cooking. It was flat on the bottom, had three legs to hold the pot's bottom above hot coals, and had a flat lid upon which to place hot coals for baking. Paul Revere has been credited by some writers with making many of the improvements of the early oven. The Dutch oven as we know it today was being born.

ITS NAME?

No one knows for sure where the name "Dutch oven" originated. Perhaps the most plausible explanation, as is reported in John Ragsdale's book, *Dutch Ovens Chronicled*, is that in 1704 English foundry owner Abraham Darby traveled to Holland to inspect casting of some brass vessels in dry sand molds. Holland had more advanced foundry technology and many thick-walled, heavy cast iron vessels were imported into Britain. From this observation, and after some experiments, Darby perfected a method to cast iron vessels in dry sand molds. In 1708 he patented the process and soon began producing a large number of cooking pots. By the mid-eighteenth century, these pots were being shipped to the colonies. They were first referred to as "Dutch pots," and later, "Dutch ovens."

Another explanation is that once the improved cast iron cooking pot became popular in America, British and New England manufacturers began producing it in large numbers. Dutch traders traveled throughout the American colonies and frontier, and peddled the pots, thus the name Dutch ovens.

There are several other theories as to how the name came about; however we will never know for sure, and while it is interesting, it is not important. The one thing that is for sure is the name stuck and has been in use for almost three centuries.

OVER THE MOUNTAINS

The Dutch oven was a much-needed and valued part of the homestead as pioneers moved toward the Appalachian Mountains. As long-hunters explored the wilderness areas "over the mountains"

The first settlers in the Appalachian mountains had no stoves, only their fireplace and Dutch ovens and/or iron skillets.

they carried the Dutch oven to use in their base camps. Historian Harriette Simpson Arnow, in her book, *Seedtime on the Cumberland*, tells about long-hunters in 1769 not having a Dutch oven large enough to cook a 40-pound wild turkey. In the book she tells the value of the Dutch oven to the settlers who first settled Tennessee and that not all of them could afford to buy ironware as it was most expensive.

Allen Eckert, writing in his book, *The Frontiersman*, tells that famous long-hunter Simon Kenton, in April of 1771, coming upon a cabin near the Ohio River, saw a woman cooking hoe-cake on an iron bake-oven lid.

Later that year, Eckert reports, Kenton and fellow explorers purchased three iron kettles to take with them to the frontier that was later called Kentucky.

LEWIS AND CLARK

In 1804, one of the greatest expeditions in history departed St. Louis to explore the United States' newly acquired Louisiana Territory. The Lewis and Clark Expedition was to be one of the most famous camping trips of all time. The cast iron Dutch oven would certainly have been one of the choice cooking vessels of the expedition, or would it?

As I write this book, the two-year bicentennial celebration of the Lewis and Clark Expedition is about to begin. There is much being written about, and promoted concerning this grand adventure, not the least of which is the cast iron Dutch ovens they used to cook dog, horse, and a wide variety of wild foods. Like many writers, in the past I have written that the Dutch oven was carried by Lewis and Clark on their trip. Did I know it for sure or did I trust

BELOW: As the explorers and settlers pushed over the mountains,
they carried their iron cookware
with them.

another writer? I trusted another modern writer. For this book I wanted to write about Dutch ovens based on solid historical facts.

I began my research by reading the published journals of the expedition written by Lewis. There was no mention of cast iron Dutch ovens. Disappointed, I next read the published journal kept by expedition member Patrick Gass, and again no mention of Dutch ovens. Could it be that the Dutch oven didn't make the trip, and over the years all of us who have written about the use of the Dutch oven on the expedition were wrong?

The next step in my research was to obtain a list of the expedition supplies Lewis purchased and search the list for cast iron Dutch ovens. Upon careful examination I found that Lewis purchased eight brass kettles, but found no mention of Dutch ovens. This was disappointing. Also, I knew of two cast iron Dutch oven manufacturers that were planning on making commemorative Dutch ovens to celebrate the expedition's use of Dutch ovens two hundred years ago. I wanted to establish that the cast iron Dutch oven went on the trip for the sake of these two companies as well as for myself.

Mountainmen of the early 1800s used Dutch ovens in their base camps and it was a popular trade good at their rendezvous.

I spent several weeks sending e-mails to anyone, and any organization, that I thought might prove to me that a Dutch oven went along on the Lewis and Clark Expedition. No one had proof and I was shocked at the number that referred me to articles I had written in past years. "My bad research was coming back to punish me," I thought.

In the summer of 2003 I attended a lecture by Professor Gary E. Moulton of the University of Nebraska. Dr. Moulton is a Lewis and Clark Expedition scholar and has researched and written more about the expedition than anyone. At the end of the lecture I had the opportunity to talk to Dr. Moulton and told him the problems I was having with my research. He smiled and said there is only one source that proves that Dutch ovens went on the expedition. "Read the journal expedition member Joseph Whitehouse kept and you will find the proof you need," Dr. Moulton told me.

I did, and it solved the mystery. Whitehouse writes of caching Dutch ovens on Tuesday, June 11, 1805. There you have it, from someone who was there: The Lewis and Clark Expedition did have Dutch ovens on their trip.

MOUNTAINMEN AND DUTCH OVENS

Soon to follow Lewis and Clark were the mountainmen. In their quest for beaver, they went into remote regions of the West where no Europeans had gone before. They took the cast iron Dutch oven with them.

While there were few mountainmen who kept a journal, there is enough recorded about their camps and activities to prove the Dutch oven was an important part of their base camps. Mountainman Osborne Russell wrote in April 1834 that their "camp kettles had not been greased for some time."

In the book *Crow Killer*, historical scholars Raymond W. Throp and Robert Bunker tell how John Johnston, the mountainman the movie *Jeremiah Johnson* was based on, saved himself and fellow trappers from attacking Blackfeet by baking biscuits in a cabin fireplace, no doubt in a Dutch oven. The biscuits were laced with strychnine. The Indians stopped to eat

Chuck wagon cooks have used Dutch ovens as an essential part of their cooking outfit since the beginning of the U.S. cattle industry.

the fresh-baked biscuits before pursuing the escaping trappers, and that saved the mountain-men. Even with this break, the men had to walk 250 miles to the safety of a fort.

In Don Holm's *Old Fashioned Dutch Oven Cookbook,* he tells about John Colter, one of the members of the Lewis and Clark Expedition who became a mountainman, dying in 1813. Colter's Dutch oven was sold for the equivalent of a week's pay, $4.00, at the executor's auction. He kept his Dutch oven to the end.

Cast iron Dutch ovens were one of the more popular trade items at the annual fur trade rendezvous, favored by mountainmen and Indians alike for cooking.

WESTERN SETTLERS

There are many accounts of Dutch ovens being listed as a necessary item for settlers moving west to have if they were to join a wagon train. The black pot was a favorite among the Mormons as they made their way to the Great Salt Lake, pulling their people-powered hand-carts. Utah history recorded that the miners digging in the canyons around Bingham, Price, and Cedar City counted on the black pots and valued them as essential as their picks.

Remote homesteaders and ranchers only had the home fireplace in which to cook, and cast iron Dutch ovens and skillets were considered some of their most valuable furnishings. Where wood was scarce dried buffalo dung, called "buffalo chips," or dried cow dung was used as a fuel source. Buffalo chips were a prized fuel source for wagon trains traveling across the Great Plains. They did not burn as long or as well as hardwood but they were better than nothing.

COWBOYS, CHUCK WAGONS, AND DUTCH OVENS

Perhaps nowhere in history did the cast iron Dutch oven play a larger role in feeding hungry workers than in the cow camps of the American West. Chuck wagon cooks demanded that their

As miners, loggers, and trappers packed into remote camps, they found it impractical to pack large, heavy iron stoves; they chose the Dutch oven as a small, lightweight alternative.

outfits include several Dutch ovens. (It's still that way today.) All you have to do to see this in action is look at the many paintings by Charles Russell and Frederic Remington of cow camps. Almost all will have Dutch ovens shown on or near the campfire. Old photos of chuck wagons and cow camps will usually show the Dutch oven in use.

DUTCH OVENS GO TO WAR

The Dutch oven was a part of cooking gear for many soldiers on both sides of the American Civil War. Rations of beans and cornmeal were quickly turned into a tasty meal using the Dutch oven. The oven could also turn local crops such as corn, peanuts, and turnip greens into a hot meal when they were on short rations.

JOSEPH LODGE BUILDS CAST IRON FOUNDRY

In 1896, Pennsylvanian Joseph Lodge built a cast iron foundry in the Cumberland Plateau foothills town of South Pittsburg, Tennessee. One of its best-known products was the Dutch oven. That insignificant foundry in the small Tennessee town is now one of the most modern cast iron cookware foundries in the world and the leading producer of cast iron Dutch ovens.

COOKING VESSEL IN EARLY 1900S WORKING CAMPS

As America grew following the First World War, various types of working camps sprung up in remote areas of North America. Mining, logging, trapping, etc. put men into locations where iron stoves were impractical. Here, it is recorded, the cast iron Dutch oven was depended upon to feed the hungry workers.

My dad worked in southern Appalachian ginseng and golden seal camps during the 1920s, and he told many stories about the Dutch ovens being used to feed the work crews that dug the valuable roots. As the depression of the early '30s belted the country he rode a horse into remote areas of the mountains and bought furs from trappers. He told of the remote camps and homesteads that used cast iron Dutch ovens as their means of cooking food.

In the late 1960s, unexpectedly, I shared a lonely high-country camp in western Wyoming with a Basque sheepherder. It was a sudden snowstorm that brought about this unusual meeting. I was scouting for a hunting party and the storm made it dangerous to return to my base camp that night. The simple sheepherder spoke with an accent, and I'm sure he thought the same of me. He welcomed me into his camp, a small enclosed sleeping wagon with a tarp cover stretched out over a cheery campfire. Off to one side of the campfire were three Dutch ovens with hot coals on their lids. He told me he was preparing his dinner, which he asked me to share with him. I really appreciated the invitation for there was no food in my saddlebags.

As we sat in his wagon and dined on a fine meal of lamb, baked potatoes, and sourdough bread, washed down with wine, he told me about his people coming to the United States beginning in the late 1800s to tend remote flocks of sheep. He had come to this country in 1950 to replace his ailing father tending sheep in this range.

Fascinated by his well-worn Dutch ovens I asked him where he got them. He proudly told me they were his grandfather's, who purchased them when he came to the United States in 1889. He said his people depended upon the heavy pots when living in the high country. The tasty dinner he served me spoke highly of the pots, and the gentleman who was my host.

SCOUTS CONTINUE THE TRADITION

As wood-burning stoves became popular, and after them modern gas and electric ranges, the Dutch oven began to fade away as a relic of the past. Fortunately for us, the Boy Scout and Girl Scout organizations recognized the value of Dutch oven cooking as a part of their camping programs and kept the art of Dutch oven cooking alive. Some of the best Dutch oven cooking tips and techniques available today come from the scouts; they really use them.

COOK-OFFS REKINDLE DUTCH OVEN COOKING

In the late 1970s and early 1980s, various cook-offs were becoming popular. Some were chuck wagon cooking competitions, others were wild game or chili cook-offs. The one thing that was

Today delicious meals can be easily prepared in Dutch ovens on patios and in parks, just as our forefathers did in their cabins and camps.

common among many of the cook-offs was the use of the cast iron Dutch oven. Soon in Utah and Texas there were Dutch oven cook-offs. From there, Dutch oven cooking became a popular means of cooking at home on the patio or on a campground.

It became so popular that in 1984 the International Dutch Oven Society (IDOS) was formed. The organization was started after the "Great American Dutch Oven Cook-off" in Logan, Utah, had been held for five years with great success. The cook-off name was changed in 1987 to the "World Championship Dutch Oven Cook-off." Today the IDOS has members from all over the United States and several countries.

At this writing there are more than seventy annual Dutch oven cook-offs in twenty-two states and each year the number grows.

OFFICIAL COOK POT OF UTAH

The people of the state of Utah think so much of the Dutch oven and the tradition of cooking in this black pot that in 1997 the state legislature enacted legislation designating the Dutch oven as the state's cooking pot. Utah is the number-one market for Dutch ovens and Dutch oven cooking has become a favorite pastime of the natives of the state. It is from this great state that much of our knowledge of Dutch oven cooks originates.

Today Dutch oven cooking has become a trendy way to cook on the patio and on campgrounds. Many are trading in their charcoal grill for one, or more, of the black pots. I live near the Talladega International Speedway, and during the latest NASCAR race one of the thousands of race fans who camp near the raceway was cooking in Dutch ovens rather than on a grill. He had so many onlookers he put up a rope barrier so he could cook.

Dutch oven cooking is being discovered by an ever-increasing number of outdoor chefs. It is a fun and delicious way to cook almost any dish and it has a touch of history that adds spice to the meal.

"I can't believe what I am seeing," Barry exclaimed as he desperately tried to pull the aluminum Dutch oven from the fire.

We were on the first day of a five-day canoe trip down the Suwannee River. For cooking, we had packed two cast iron Dutch ovens and an aluminum Dutch oven in which to bake bread. In our haste to set up our first camp, my friend Barry had put the ingredients for a quick stew in a standard aluminum Dutch oven. To speed things up, he had placed the oven in the hot coals of our campfire. Then he placed a shovelful of hot coals on the lid.

As he helped with camp chores, a brisk wind blew through the campsite. The campfire coals glowed brightly. When he finally got around to checking on the stew he found the aluminum Dutch oven changing shape and the lid depositing hot pieces of molten aluminum into the stew. Needless to say, a lesson was learned that night, and we had peanut butter and jelly sandwiches for dinner.

When most outdoor cooks think of Dutch ovens they think of the heavy cast iron Dutch ovens. However there are quality cast aluminum Dutch ovens, such as those made by GSI Outdoors, that have their place in outdoor cooking, provided you know their advantages and limitations. As I write this, GSI is introducing a line of new hard-anodized aluminum Dutch ovens that hold a lot of promise as they heat more evenly than standard aluminum Dutch ovens and they have a non-stick surface.

The aluminum Dutch oven vs. the cast iron Dutch oven: you be the judge.

ADVANTAGES OF THE ALUMINUM DUTCH OVEN

There are several advantages that aluminum Dutch ovens have over their cast iron counterparts. But remember the old axiom: you must give up something to get something. Here are the advantages:

When light weight is a must, the aluminum oven can be
counted on to produce good meals.

Lightweight:

First and foremost, they are lightweight. An empty 12-inch aluminum oven will weigh
about 7 pounds; the same size cast iron oven will weigh about 18 pounds. Quickly that
tells you the aluminum model is more desirable when lightweight packing is a must. Also
its light weight is an advantage when you pick up an oven full of food. Aluminum is a good
choice for cooks with physical limitations.

Rustproof:

The aluminum oven doesn't rust, thus you do not have to be as concerned about leaving
it damp or storing it for long periods. I have seen poorly seasoned cast iron Dutch ovens
rust overnight when left out in the dew.

Seasoning not required:

Since aluminum does not rust, you do not have to pre-season the oven as you do a cast
iron oven. However, food will tend to stick to an unseasoned aluminum oven and some
cooks pre-season their aluminum ovens for that reason. Breaking in an aluminum oven

The new GSI hard-anodized aluminum ovens hold a lot of promise for those who want a heat-holding lightweight Dutch oven.

is simply a process of giving it a good washing to remove the protective oil coating put on by the manufacturer. The new hard cast aluminum ovens have a non-stick surface.

Easier to clean:

Unseasoned aluminum ovens can be cleaned by washing with soap and hot water. It makes for a quick and easy cleanup.

Does not discolor food:

Cast iron Dutch ovens, especially those not properly seasoned, can turn foods such as beans a dark color. Aluminum will not do this.

Heats quicker:

Aluminum ovens heat quicker than cast iron ovens, requiring less preheating time.

One of the real masters of Dutch oven cooking is George Prechter III. You will find me quoting George many times in this book. He is a well-known New Orleans chef and cooking writer who has studied Dutch oven cooking for many years. George states, "The aluminum Dutch oven is a valuable cooking vessel where lightweight is a must and the cook is well trained in the proper use of an aluminum oven. I like them for baking bread and making gravies."

ADVANTAGES OF CAST IRON DUTCH OVENS

Cast iron Dutch ovens are steeped in history and tradition, and a large number of Dutch oven cooks prefer the advantages of cast iron over aluminum. Here are the advantages most often given:

Long Lasting:

Cast iron ovens are famous for lasting generations and becoming family heirlooms. Many around today are well over one hundred years old. During the pioneering days of early America the family cast iron Dutch oven was valuable enough to be included in wills. John Rutledge, writing in his excellent book, *Dutch Ovens Chronicled*, tells of Mary Washington, mother of General George Washington, wanting to be certain her cast iron vessels were cared for. In her will, dated May 20, 1788, she provided that half of her "iron kitchen furniture" would go to a grandson, Fielding Lewis, and the other half would go to a granddaughter, Betty Carter. Rutledge states, "Surely there were several Dutch ovens among her iron kitchen furniture." Most Dutch oven cooks will be quick to tell you that the older a cast iron oven gets, the better it cooks.

Distributes heat evenly:

While cast iron ovens take a little longer than aluminum to heat up, the heat is distributed evenly, resulting in fewer "hot spots" producing and giving ideal cooking conditions. If your food burns, you got the oven too hot. Less heat is needed with cast iron.

Retains heat:

Cast iron ovens, once heated to a desired temperature, are easier than aluminum to keep at that temperature. Cast iron ovens require less fuel and time refueling.

Heavy lid seals in steam:

The heavy, tight-fitting lid of a cast iron Dutch oven helps hold steam in, so the oven acts as a pressure cooker and helps keep food tender and moist.

Nutritional benefits:

Cooking in cast iron Dutch ovens is healthful, as cast iron cookware imparts a significant amount of dietary iron to your food, which is absorbed by the body.

Tolerates Higher Heat:

No Dutch oven should be subjected to high temperatures, but on occasion it does happen, as I wrote at the beginning of this chapter. When it does, the cast iron oven stands a better chance of surviving the event, as aluminum will melt at around 1175° Fahrenheit. Cast iron melts at around 2200° Fahrenheit. Wind-blown coals and campfires can generate temperatures in those ranges. Also, cast iron heats more slowly without sudden temperature flare-ups so that the food is protected from burning longer.

So which type Dutch oven is best? Most experienced Dutch oven cooks will agree that, with the exception of weight, the cast iron oven is the top choice. That is not to say you can't prepare good meals with an aluminum Dutch oven; you can, and the new hard-anodized aluminum ovens may have additional qualities similar to cast iron, but for total satisfaction you can't beat cast iron. Most Dutch oven cooks have to agree with George Prechter when he answered an interviewer asking about his choice in Dutch ovens: "If given a choice and weight is not a factor, I will choose a cast iron Dutch oven almost every time."

One of the merits of the aluminum oven is it is rustproof.

The cast iron oven has stood the test of time, over two centuries of testing, and is still the favorite among Dutch oven chefs.

CHAPTER THREE

According to Bob Kellermann at Lodge Manufacturing Company, the process for making cast iron hasn't really changed in six hundred years. It is the equipment, production speed, and quality of the final product that have been enhanced through technology. Where there were once coke-fired cupolas to bring the iron to its molten state now there is electric induction melting. It offers greater quality control and is significantly cleaner. In the past, each Dutch oven was molded and poured by hand.

Today, automatic molding machines do it all. They are faster and yield more consistent product quality. Bob told me these facts when I visited the Lodge foundry in South Pittsburg, Tennessee, to see for myself how quality Dutch ovens were made.

Many serious Dutch oven cooks I have been around dream of a trip to Lodge to see how Dutch ovens are made. I know of one championship-winning chuck wagon cook who took his wife on a vacation to Tennessee just so they could visit the Dutch oven manufacturing company.

While working on this book, Kellermann invited me to visit Lodge and go onto the foundry floor to watch Dutch ovens being made. The trip gave me a whole new respect for quality Dutch ovens and I still wonder why they don't cost several hundred dollars apiece.

Here, in brief, are the steps that go into making a cast iron Dutch oven:

First, a pattern of the Dutch oven is made. This is the reverse image of the product, with a runner system or small trough built into the pattern. This will allow the molten metal to flow into the pattern to form the Dutch oven.

New Dutch ovens on their way to be packaged for shipping.

The pattern is mounted on a molding machine that squeezes sand under extremely high pressure to form the mold. Each piece of cast iron cookware is formed in its own mold. High-quality sand is washed, dried, and mixed by grain fineness to Lodge specifications prior to delivery. Lodge tests the quality of the sand throughout production in a state-of-the-art sand lab.

Molten iron at 2800° Fahrenheit is poured into the cavity left by the pattern. Iron melts at approximately 2000° Fahrenheit but Lodge heats it an additional 800° Fahrenheit for maximum fluidity and smoothest pouring. The iron used must meet stringent Lodge standards. Today, with an amazing piece of equipment called a Spectrometer, Lodge is able to test the elemental make-up of the iron and monitor for consistency during production.

After the metal cools and solidifies to form a casting, it is mechanically removed from the sand.

The sand used to make the casting is recycled—reduced to grain size, re-coated with clay and water, and reintroduced to the molding machine to be used again. Half the metal poured to make the Dutch oven is in the runner system mentioned above. That metal is recycled back to the furnace. Roughly 110 tons of recycled sand and 6 tons of iron are used each hour of production.

The complete removal of sand baked on a casting at 2800° Fahrenheit takes some force. Abrasive steel shot is catapulted at the Dutch oven until it is cleaned.

The rough edges from the casting process are ground smooth.

The Dutch oven enters an eight-minute stone wash media bath that deburrs any sharp edges left over from grinding.

It is rinsed in water and dipped in a non-toxic, water soluble, rust-inhibiting, food-grade wax for protection while being shipped.

Once dried, the Dutch oven is sent to packaging, segregated from other types of products, labeled, packaged, loaded on pallets, and put in inventory.

One of the things that impressed me the most during my visit was that during every step of the process of making a Dutch oven, each employee acts as a quality-control inspector. If imperfections or slight blemishes are found, the product is removed from the line.

As I said in the beginning, I don't see why these quality-made ovens aren't priced at several hundred dollars. I am just glad that, thanks to modern, highly efficient machinery and management, quality Dutch ovens are still affordable and long lasting.

LEFT: Molten iron is poured into a cavity left by the Dutch oven pattern.

BELOW LEFT: Cast iron products are dipped into a non-toxic rust-inhibiting, food-grade wax for protection while being shipped.

BELOW RIGHT: Each employee at Lodge acts as a quality control inspector, checking each Dutch oven as it is produced and packaged.

Shopping for a cast iron Dutch oven can be an easy experience for the "old hand" at Dutch oven cooking, or an ordeal for someone who is new to this method of cooking. The more experienced cook knows what size he wants, whether or not he wants one pre-seasoned, what to look for to see if he is getting a quality oven, and where to shop to get the best deals. The neophyte cook must have some guidance if he is to make the right decisions in making his purchase. The following should make shopping for a Dutch oven easier for everybody.

NEW OVEN

Let's start by identifying where you can purchase new Dutch ovens. With the growing interest in Dutch oven cooking today, it is not too difficult to find retail stores that display and sell the ovens. I have found them in Wal-Mart stores throughout the country. Many camp supply shops, hardware stores, and Boy Scout supply stores carry them. Lodge Manufacturing Co. has a growing number of factory outlet stores that are not only a Dutch oven cook's dream store but offer some great prices as well.

If you want to order online or by mail, you can go directly to Lodge Manufacturing Co., Camp Chef, MACA Supply Co., or GSI Outdoors. Also, catalog supply houses such as Chuckwagon Supply, Cabela's, or Kampers Kettle carry a complete line of Dutch oven cooking supplies. Their web and mailing addresses are listed on page 141 of this book. Remember, cast iron Dutch ovens are heavy: a 10-inch oven weighs 14 pounds and a 16-inch oven weighs 35 pounds, so if you order one, expect the shipping cost to be in the $10 to $20 range; larger ovens cost much more.

When shopping for a new Dutch oven you will want to beware of cheap ovens. Cheap ovens are usually imported ovens, poorly cast or with flaws. Since you are buying a Dutch oven to give years of service, you want to buy quality. Paying a

Many hardware and outdoor stores now carry Dutch ovens.

Dutch ovens are available in a variety of sizes. Here are the author's ovens, ranging from a 5-inch oven on top to a 16-inch on the bottom.

few extra dollars to get a quality Dutch oven amounts to only a few cents a year when you amortize it over the long life of a good oven. Avoid cheap ovens; they only lead to disappointing meals.

USED DUTCH OVENS

Used Dutch ovens occasionally show up at yard sales and in secondhand stores. I have seen a number in antique stores but these were often priced as high as a new oven. Several times I have had visitors to my home offer to buy my modern Dutch ovens thinking the well-seasoned pots were real antiques.

While many used Dutch ovens have seen a life of hard knocks and neglect, some are well-seasoned ovens that have a lot of life left in them, and are available for just a few dollars. I stopped at a yard sale in Maine one summer and saw three 12-inch seasoned Dutch ovens on sale for $3.00 each. The owner just wanted to get rid of the heavy pots.

SELECTING AN OVEN

Regardless of whether you are shopping for a new or used cast iron Dutch oven, the pointers to use in selecting a quality oven are about the same.

First, be sure you know a "camp" or "outdoor" Dutch oven when you see one. I have seen a number of first-time Dutch oven cooks go to a store and purchase the wrong type of Dutch oven for cooking over coals or charcoal. While these flat-bottomed, domed-lid cast iron "kitchen" ovens are really effective for stove or grill top cooking; they

Notice the difference between the camp Dutch oven on the right and the "kitchen" oven.

are not for cooking over and under hot coals.

The "camp" or "outdoor" Dutch oven will have a flat bottom with three short, two-inch legs. These legs are to keep the bottom of the pot from touching hot coals. The pot will have a strong wire bail handle to support the oven over a fire or to use in moving the oven when hot. The lid will be flat with a rim flanged so that hot coals will stay on the lid while cooking. In the center of the lid there will be a small loop handle that enables the cook to lift the lid with a lid lifter.

You will need to give some thought to the size Dutch oven for which you may want to shop. Dutch ovens come in a wide variety of sizes. Most companies refer to their ovens by the size of the diameter of its rim. They range from 5 inches to 22 inches. The depth of a standard Dutch oven is about 3 to $3^1/_2$ inches. Some people refer to these as "bread" ovens as they are ideal for baking breads, pies, cakes, and other pastries. They are the most popular depth of Dutch ovens. Ovens designed for cooking larger dishes such as whole chickens, large amounts of stew or chili, hams, or standing rib roasts have a depth of about 5 inches and are called "meat" or "deep" Dutch ovens.

MACA Supply Co. is best known for making cast iron and aluminum Dutch ovens that are deep. Their 9-inch oven is 6 inches deep and their 22-inch oven is $9^1/_2$ inches deep. Those in-between are from $6^1/_2$ inches to 9 inches deep.

Camp Chef makes unique seasoned cast iron Dutch ovens that have a deeper lid with three short legs on it so that it can be easily used as a skillet. The lid depth on the 10-inch model is 1 inch, 12-inch model is $1^3/_8$ inches deep and the 14-inch model is $1^7/_8$ inches deep. Also, the pots are deeper by 4 inches, $4^1/_2$ inches, and 5 inches, respectively.

Lodge Manufacturing Co. makes cast iron Dutch ovens in sizes from 8 inches up to 16 inches, both shallow and deep. Their 8-inch diameter oven is 3 inches deep, 10-inch oven $3^1/_2$ inches deep, 12-inch oven $3^3/_4$ inches deep, 12-inch oven 5 inches deep, 14-inch oven $3^3/_4$ inches deep, 14-inch oven 5 inches deep, and 16-inch oven $4^1/_4$ inches deep.

Use this chart to help you select which size Dutch oven you want, based on the amount of food you will be cooking and the number of people you will serve. Keep in mind that most experienced Dutch oven cooks never try to cook an entire meal with one oven. They have several ovens in various sizes in order to cook several dishes at one time.

SELECTING A DUTCH OVEN

Oven size	Oven capacity	Persons served	Weight (pounds)
5-INCH	1 PINT	1	5
8-INCH	2 QUARTS	2–4	11
10-INCH	4 QUARTS	4–7	15
12-INCH	6 QUARTS	12–14	20
12-INCH DEEP	8 QUARTS	16–20	23
14-INCH	8 QUARTS	16–20	26
14-INCH DEEP	10 QUARTS	22–28	28
16-INCH	12 QUARTS	22–28	35

Courtesy of Lodge Manufacturing Co.

SEASONED OR UNSEASONED?

Thanks to modern technology, you have a choice today when shopping for a new Dutch oven as to whether you want it seasoned or unseasoned (sometimes called "natural finish"). If you are in a hurry to use the new oven or don't want the chore of seasoning a new oven, then you may want to purchase a seasoned oven. A seasoned oven will cost $6 to $10 more.

If you are like many of us who use Dutch ovens regularly, and enjoy the seasoning process, then you may opt for an unseasoned oven. Even if you elect to purchase a seasoned oven, be sure to learn the seasoning process as you will probably need to use the skill later.

INSPECT, INSPECT, INSPECT!!

When purchasing a new or used Dutch oven, if at all possible inspect the pot and lid carefully. Start with the pot and look for cracks, chips, casting imperfections (rare in new U.S.-made cast iron but sometimes found in cheap imports), and deep rust spots. Be sure to look on the inside and outside.

Always inspect the lid on a Dutch oven for fit.

Next, examine the lid for the same types of flaws. Finally, and perhaps most important, make sure the lid fits the pot it is paired with. It should sit squarely on the rim of the pot if heat transfer is to occur from the lid to the side of the pot. Push on the rim of the lid all around and make sure there is no rocking motion. Also make sure the lid does not fit too tightly, as the lid can get stuck on the pot during seasoning or cooking. I have seen lids that were too tight become frozen on the pot during cooking, requiring a lot of effort at mealtime to get them off, often resulting in a broken lid or pot. I like about $^1/_8$-inch side motion to a lid. A properly fitting lid forms a seal when cooking that creates pressure and aids in keeping the dish being cooked moist. I have seen people who got a good buy on a used Dutch oven, with an ill-fitting lid solve the problem by smearing valve-compound on the rim of the pot and the edge of the lid, and then rotating the lid until they had a proper fit.

Tight-fitting lids are usually found on cheap imports or on used Dutch ovens when a matching lid was lost or broken and a lid from another oven replaced it.

Finally, always check the wire bail on a used oven to make sure it is strong enough to allow the user to pick up the oven full of food without breaking or coming loose. It is a surprise to new Dutch oven cooks to learn just how heavy a cast iron oven full of food is. A 12-inch oven full of food can weigh as much as 25 pounds. Lifting it off the coals by the wire bail is not the time to discover a weak bail.

Inspect wire bails on used Dutch ovens. When you are lifting an oven full of food is a poor time to discover a weak bail.

Two of the most common problems new Dutch oven cooks have with their cast iron pots are: **1.** seasoning them correctly the first time and **2.** re-seasoning them after hard use.

REASONS TO SEASON

Cast iron is very porous, and there are several reasons to season a cast iron Dutch oven. The seasoning process creates a patina that keeps food from sticking to the sides, bottom, and lid of the vessel. Thanks to this sheen it is quicker and easier to clean. It also protects the vessel from rusting. An unseasoned (also called "natural finish") cast iron oven can rust overnight just from the moisture in the air. The third reason to season an oven, and by far not the least important, is that it adds a flavor to the foods cooked in the oven that is unmatched in other types of cookware.

The theory behind seasoning cast iron is that oil will fill the tiny holes in the oven. The oil, when heated, will form a carbon non-stick coating on the Dutch oven. The oven will darken with each use and the patina will improve with each use to turn your oven into the ultimate non-stick vessel. A well-seasoned Dutch oven will be black.

PRE-SEASONED OVENS MAY NOW BE PURCHASED

Today, Lodge Dutch ovens may be purchased pre-seasoned. It is a process they call Lodge Logic. Lodge Logic is a process whereby Dutch ovens are electrostatically coated with a proprietary vegetable oil and cured at high temperatures to allow the oil to deeply penetrate the surface of the cast iron. It's ready to use when you purchase the Dutch oven.

As I was writing this book I also received word that Camp Chef would be shipping all its Advantage cast iron Dutch ovens pre-seasoned.

Even if you purchase these pre-seasoned ovens, chances are good you will need

A gas grill is one of the best tools to use in seasoning a Dutch oven.

Compare the color of the unseasoned oven on the left to the seasoned oven on the right.

to re-season them sometime in the future. Be sure to follow the manufacturer's instructions when you first clean the new oven so as not to destroy the seasoning.

CLEAN A NEW DUTCH OVEN FIRST

New unseasoned Dutch ovens are usually coated during the manufacturing process with a wax coating to protect them during travel to the retailer's shelves. When you get a new oven home remove all stickers and wash it with mild dishwashing liquid to remove the wax coating. Rinse and dry it thoroughly. Season it immediately or the oven will rust at an amazing speed. Never cook in a Dutch oven without first seasoning it.

SEASONING A DUTCH OVEN

While some Dutch oven cooks look at the seasoning process as work, I look at it as a ritual where I get to know the new oven, and I feel that I play a small role in the success of many future meals. Here are several ways you can season or re-season your Dutch ovens.

To season a new cast iron Dutch oven and I know many cooks who season their aluminum ovens as well start by preheating your home oven to 350°. Open some windows and turn off the smoke detector as some smoke may be created by this process. Place the pot and lid in the oven and heat until they are almost too hot to handle. This opens the pores of the cast iron. Remove the pot and lid and, using a paper towel, rub a thin layer of liquid olive or vegetable oil or solid vegetable shortening I use solid Crisco on the inside and outside of the pot and lid. (Camp Chef has a product called Cast Iron Conditioner that also serves this purpose.) Do not use margarine or butter. Cover all surfaces, including the legs. Be sure not to coat the surface too thickly. Keep the coats very thin. I know of one Dutch oven cook that set his oven on fire because he used thick layers of lard to season his Dutch ovens.

Place the Dutch oven and lid on the top rack of your preheated kitchen oven. Be sure to put aluminum foil or better yet a cookie sheet on the lower rack of the oven to catch any excess oil. Not only does this help keep the oven clean, it protects the oven from drippings that could cause an oven fire.

Some people like to use spray oil to season their ovens, but I find it can leave a sticky coat-

ing. I have also tried lard and found it turns rancid during long periods of storage.

Bake the oven and lid for one hour. Turn the kitchen oven off and let the Dutch oven cool down to handling temperature. Repeat the process. Remove the pot and lid from the oven and wipe it out with a clean, dry cloth. Your Dutch oven is seasoned and ready for use.

If you don't want to run the risk of smoking up your home kitchen, there are several outdoor methods of seasoning your Dutch oven.

The first, and perhaps the easiest, is to simply have a fish fry and use your Dutch oven as a deep fryer. Frying several batches of fish, hush puppies, and French fried potatoes will fill the pores of the cast iron with vegetable oil. Once the cooking is over, pour out the oil and wipe the pot and lid clean with a paper towel.

I have a friend who lives in the bush of British Columbia and uses Dutch ovens almost daily. He seasons a new Dutch oven by frying thick-sliced, unsalted bacon in the pot and on the lid for several months. It works. His Dutch ovens have a beautiful black patina.

LEFT PAGE: The home oven can be used
to season a Dutch oven as long as some
precautions are taken.

An outdoor method I like that doesn't smoke up your kitchen is to use a propane gas cooking grill, which has a cover. Turn the grill on *low* and place the Dutch oven in the grill to preheat. When it becomes warm, remove the Dutch oven and wipe on a thin layer of vegetable oil, Camp Chef Cast Iron Conditioner, or shortening. Place the lid and oven in the grill and turn the grill to *low*. Lower the grill lid. Cook for one hour. Repeat the process. Remove the oven and lid and wipe it out with a clean, dry cloth. I have friends who use the same method using a charcoal grill. Be careful not to overheat the Dutch oven.

RE-SEASONING AN OVEN

One of the major reasons cast iron Dutch ovens need to be re-seasoned is that they are often improperly cleaned. Harsh detergents and scrubbings with metal scrapers can do damage to an oven's seasoning. Be sure to read the chapter in this book about cleaning the oven the correct way.

Other reasons Dutch ovens need to be re-seasoned are if they become rusted or are improperly stored and the oil turns rancid. Regardless of the reason, the way to re-season a cast iron Dutch oven is identical to the method for a new one, starting with a very clean pot and lid, and repeating one of the above procedures.

Once your Dutch oven is seasoned, never use strong soap, harsh detergent, metal scouring pads, metal scrapers, or the dishwasher for cleaning. This destroys the seasoning, requiring you to go through the seasoning process again.

The author prefers to season his ovens with Crisco.

CHAPTER SIX

I t comes as a surprise to most first-time cast iron Dutch oven cooks that their seasoned ovens are so easy to clean. It is much easier to clean a seasoned Dutch oven than it is to scrub most conventional cooking pots and pans. In fact, if there is a problem with cleaning a Dutch oven, it is that too much cleaning is done. The result is an oven that needs to be re-seasoned.

Cleaning the cast iron Dutch oven is a three-step process:

1. Remove Food:

Using a wooden or plastic spoon, natural fiber or plastic scrub brush, or plastic or natural fiber scouring pad, scrape out all food. *Never* use a metal scraper or steel wool or wire scouring pad and *never* wash in a dishwasher, as this will ruin the pot's seasoning.

Many Dutch oven cooks say never to wash a seasoned oven and lid with soap, as it will ruin the seasoning and give the food cooked in the oven a soapy taste. I have found that a well-seasoned oven can be washed with warm water and a *mild* dishwashing soap without negative results. Be sure to rinse well with warm water.

If you have cooked something that has stuck to the oven and is difficult to remove, partially fill the oven with clean, warm water and bring the water to a boil. Brush while boiling. Most stuck food will come off when boiled. If not, scour with a plastic scouring pad or plastic-bristle brush. Never pour cold water into a hot oven, or hot water into a cold oven, as it can cause permanent damage to the oven. I once saw a cook, cleaning a very hot oven, pour cold water into it. The pot cracked and it was ruined.

Once all food is out of the oven and off the underside of the lid, rinse the pot and lid in warm water.

A great way to store Dutch ovens is at home as fireplace decorations.

2. Dry:

Immediately after the oven has been rinsed, using a paper or clean cloth towel, dry the entire oven and lid. Many cooks dry their ovens by placing them on heat until they are hot to the touch. The point is, you want your oven as dry as possible to prevent rust. Once the oven and lid are dry, you will want to oil them lightly, at once, for long-term protection from rust.

3. Oil:

Lightly coat the entire oven and lid, inside and out, with vegetable, mineral, or olive oil. Be careful not to get the oil coating too thick as it will become a gummy mess in time. Also, a thick coating of oil will turn rancid quickly. Do not use lard for oiling, as it will turn rancid in a short period of time. In fact, most oils will turn rancid during periods of long storage, especially if the oven is stored with the lid on tight. Food cooked in a rancid pot will taste the way the pot smells. I like to use mineral oil for long-term storage, as I have never had it turn rancid when my ovens were properly stored.

LEFT PAGE: Care should be used
in cleaning a seasoned cast iron
oven. Use only a soft brush or
scrub pad.

Dutch ovens should be cleaned as quickly as possible after cooking a dish in them: the sooner the better. Never use a Dutch oven for storing food, as the acid in foods will quickly penetrate the seasoning on the utensil, allowing the cast iron to come in direct contact with water causing rust to appear when it is washed and dried. Never allow your oven to sit in water, or water to stand on it. A cast iron Dutch oven will rust before your eyes if you don't protect it from moisture.

STORAGE

Since most Dutch ovens go for long periods without being used, proper storage techniques are important for the oven to protect it from rusting or turning rancid.

First, select a place to store your ovens that is protected from moisture and dust. Where I live in Alabama, a Dutch oven stored in an enclosed garage or outside storage room will be subject to rusting rapidly, due to our high humidity. I like to store my Dutch ovens in the family room as fireplace decorations. In the house, the central heat and air conditioning keep the humidity under control.

Regardless of where you store your Dutch ovens, *never* store them with the lid on tight. That will almost guarantee that moisture will condense on the inside and rust the pot. Also, the lack of air circulation will cause most oil coatings to turn rancid.

To properly store your Dutch oven, place the lid on the pot, using a spacer to keep the lid ajar to allow air movement. A couple of sheets of rolled up paper towels can serve this purpose. Some people use a small roll of aluminum foil as a spacer. You want a good exchange of air between the inside of the pot and the outside.

Some people go one step further and place a piece of real charcoal—not charcoal briquet—wrapped up in a paper towel inside the oven. This absorbs odor and moisture.

DEALING WITH RUST

Rust is an enemy of cast iron, and even the most cared-for Dutch ovens can develop rust spots. The first rule in dealing with rust is to examine your oven regularly for rust spots. Be sure to look inside and out and examine the lid thoroughly. The sooner you find rust, the better. Over

Coke can be used to clean rusted cast iron. The photo on the left is before cleaning.

a period of time rust can ruin the oven and it can happen quicker than you might believe.

When rust is found on your Dutch oven it should be dealt with immediately. First remove the rust with a wire brush or steel wool. To save some elbow grease, some cooks soak the rusty area in Coca-Cola for a couple of hours then scrub the rust away using a wire brush.

Once the rust has been removed it will be necessary to re-season the pot or lid according to the instructions given in chapter five.

TRANSPORTING A DUTCH OVEN

Dutch ovens have a way of traveling a lot. It may be to a friend's house for a backyard cook-out, on a family camping trip, in the RV, on a canoe trip, or to the family cabin. Regardless of where it is going, the oven needs to be packed for the trip so that the oven and those items it comes in contact with are protected. I was once on a canoe trip when an improperly packed Dutch oven leg went through the canoe bottom, causing a major leak. I have seen Dutch ovens being unloaded from a vehicle dropped on concrete and broken. I have seen them break lantern globes in a station wagon cargo area. They need to be transported so that the oven and surroundings are protected.

Many Dutch oven cooks purchase specially designed padded Dutch oven transporting bags, such as the Camp Gourmet Dutch Oven Case available from GSI or the Camp Dutch Oven Tote Bag from Lodge Manufacturing Co. These are a good investment if your Dutch oven is to be transported.

Transporting a Dutch oven is best done with a padded carrying case, such as these GSI cases.

Other cooks build lidded wooden boxes to fit their Dutch ovens. They work well but are heavy when the oven is in them. Some keep the cardboard box the oven came in when they bought it, but it usually doesn't last long. Whatever you use, treat your ovens and the items around them with care when transporting them. Allow them to bounce around without protection and the oven, as well as other items, will become damaged.

When I first started cooking in a Dutch oven I had few accessories: a fireplace poker with a crook in it was used as a lid lifter and whatever shovel was available was used to shovel hot coals from the campfire. While they worked, using them was far from perfection and there were many burned fingers, sometimes burned food, and often unknown meal completion times.

With the many wonderful accessories that are available to the Dutch oven cook today there is little reason to have the problems I had when I first started. In fact, the novice Dutch oven cook today can start out cooking like an expert, thanks to the accessories available. They allow him to get a fire going quickly, to handle the ovens safely, control the fire with ease, cook at a comfortable height, and keep the oven clean. What our ancestors would have given for these accessories!

COOKING TABLE

Today, far more Dutch oven cooking is being done in backyards and parks than in the backcountry and around campfires. Most of it is done using charcoal rather than coals from an open fire. To accommodate cooks using charcoal, someone came up with the idea of a steel table upon which to cook. It put the ovens at a comfortable height, which made cooking much easer when compared to bending over ovens on the ground. The table made it easy to position the charcoal briquets and was easy to clean up after use. Also, the table saved yards and parks from burn spots caused by charcoal placed on the ground for cooking.

As the cooking table continued to evolve, innovations were added to make the table more user-friendly. Removable windscreens were added, which helped make cooking time predictable on cold or windy days. Then someone came up with the idea of folding legs, which made the table easy to store and pack. Adjustable legs

A long-handled shovel keeps your hands away from the heat when moving hot coals.

Dutch oven cooking table

were added, which makes the table adjustable for uneven cooking sites.

The cooking table I use, the Camp Dutch Oven Cooking Table made by Lodge Manufacturing Co., has all of these features. It is all steel, weighs 40 pounds, folds flat for easy carrying and storage, and can be set up within a minute or so. The tabletop measures 26 x 16 x 32 in. and can accommodate two to four Dutch ovens, depending upon the sizes being used and whether or not stack cooking is being done.

Other companies that offer Dutch oven cooking tables include Camp Chef, Cabela's, and Chuckwagon Supply.

Keep a whisk broom and scraper, such as a putty knife, with the table to help with the table cleanup.

Dutch oven with rack and heavy-duty aluminum cake pan, shown at right in position.

CAKE RACKS AND CAKE PANS

During my early days of Dutch oven cooking I was like many beginners and questioned whether all the work that can go into cooking was worth it. There was the constant cleanup of the oven, I had to watch what I cooked, as some high-acid foods required that I re-season the oven occasionally, and I was still burning some dishes no matter how hard I tried to master cooking in the black pot.

This all changed when I was on a hunt in a remote camp in Montana where the camp cook used cake racks and heavy-duty cake pans in his Dutch ovens and simply used the ovens like a home oven. Since the cake pans containing food were on the racks he had no burned foods. The racks allowed for good air circulation and eliminated hot spots. The heavy-duty aluminum cake pans kept the food away from the oven so cleanup was a snap. Rarely did he have to re-season a Dutch oven.

When I came home I went to a restaurant supply store and purchased cake racks and heavy-duty Parrish aluminum cake pans to fit inside each of my ovens. For my 12-inch shallow oven, I bought a 10-inch round cake rack and a round 9-inch, 2-inch-deep cake pan. For my 12-inch-deep Dutch oven, I bought a 10-inch cake rack and a round 9-inch, 4-inch-deep cake pan. The smaller-diameter cake pan allows room for the pan lifter to grip the pan for removal from a hot oven.

I also purchased a heavy-duty professional-size pan lifter that makes lifting an aluminum pan of food out of a hot oven easy. It is almost impossible to remove a hot cake pan full of food from a hot Dutch oven without the lifter.

I now use this cake rack/cake pan combination for many recipes in all of my ovens and it has cut down on much of the work I used to do when Dutch-oven cooking. With the aluminum pans, I don't have to worry when I cook beans or dishes with high-acid content, like tomatoes. I also use it with dishes that have a lot of sugar in them to help with the cleanup. Other than an occasional spillover, the food never touches the cast iron. I am now seeing more chuck wagon cooks use this method of cooking, and for good reason.

Also, I have added several loft pans to my outfit. I can cook two dishes at once by using two loft pans, on a cake rack, in my larger ovens. They are nice for dishes like meat loafs and cobblers.

Parrish, and other heavy-duty aluminum round cake pans can be found by doing a search on the web. Also, most restaurant supply dealers have them. The same supplier should have pot lifters as well.

The downside to using cake pans in your Dutch ovens is that it will cut down on the amount of food you can cook at one time, compared to filling an oven without a cake rack and pan. I don't always use cake pans; there are many dishes that I like to cook in a bare oven.

Lid lifter

LID LIFTER

The lid lifter is a combination tool. It enables the cook to lift a hot and heavy Dutch oven lid, with hot ashes on it, without it swinging. Also, it enables the cook to lift the entire oven by catching the wire bail and pulling the oven up. This is one of the Dutch oven cook's most valuable tools available where ever Dutch ovens are sold.

Charcoal chimney starter

CHARCOAL CHIMNEY STARTER

I wish I had known about the charcoal chimney starter many years ago. It saves a lot of time getting charcoal to a cooking temperature and does not require starter fuel. It is simply a metal chimney in which the charcoal briquets are stacked. A sheet or two of newspaper is wadded up in the bottom and set on fire. In just a few minutes you have briquets ready to place under and on top of your Dutch oven. I see these inexpensive starters for sale in home improvement stores, and Lodge Manfacturing Co. has them as well.

LID STAND

The lid stand is made from heavy steel bar stock. It is designed to give the cook a clean stand upon which to place the Dutch oven lid when opening up the Dutch oven. A great second use for the lid stand is to put hot charcoal briquets around the stand and place a Dutch oven lid upside down on the stand for use as a griddle. Frying eggs, meats, or fish on the inverted lid is just as easy as using a frying pan. It works really well on a steel cooking table. A third use for the lid stand is pre-heating the lid for those recipes that call for a pre-heated oven. Place a few coals under the lid stand and place the lid on it. In just a few minutes you have a pre-heated lid.

Lid stand

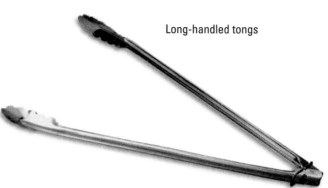

Long-handled tongs

LONG-HANDLED TONGS

In order to accurately and safely place and move hot charcoal briquet, I like to use stainless steel tongs that have long handles. The ones I like have 16-inch handles that make placing briquets quick and easy. They are also good for moving food around in a hot oven. I keep two sets of tongs in my cook outfit, one for moving briquets and one for food. They are sold at most places that sell Dutch ovens.

HEAVY LEATHER GLOVES

When Dutch oven cooking, almost everything you touch is hot, and splashing hot oil comes with the territory. To prevent burns, a pair of welding gloves or gloves made for Dutch oven cooking should be available to the cook. The gloves I use are designed for Dutch oven cooking and are sold by Lodge Manufacturing Co. They have saved my hands many unnecessary burns.

TRIPOD

If your Dutch oven cooking involves cooking over a camp-fire, you will want to have a sturdy tripod as a part of your gear. I like

Heavy leather gloves

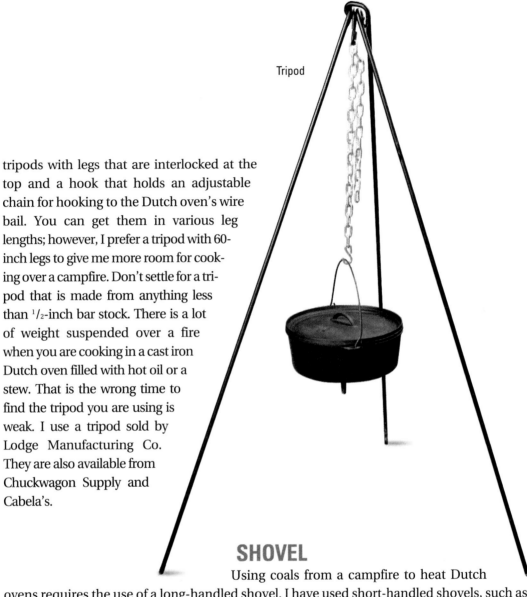

Tripod

tripods with legs that are interlocked at the top and a hook that holds an adjustable chain for hooking to the Dutch oven's wire bail. You can get them in various leg lengths; however, I prefer a tripod with 60-inch legs to give me more room for cooking over a campfire. Don't settle for a tripod that is made from anything less than $1/2$-inch bar stock. There is a lot of weight suspended over a fire when you are cooking in a cast iron Dutch oven filled with hot oil or a stew. That is the wrong time to find the tripod you are using is weak. I use a tripod sold by Lodge Manufacturing Co. They are also available from Chuckwagon Supply and Cabela's.

SHOVEL

Using coals from a campfire to heat Dutch ovens requires the use of a long-handled shovel. I have used short-handled shovels, such as the military entrenching tool, on canoe or horseback trips, but they put your hands uncomfortably close to the fire. Most cooks depend on the standard pointed work shovel that is available at any hardware store. The serious Dutch oven cook may drill holes in the shovel so that all small coals and ashes can be shaken out in the fire, delivering the larger, more desirable coals to the Dutch ovens.

Whisk broom

WHISK BROOM

Because Dutch oven cooking involves the use of coals on the lid of the vessel, at some point you need to get rid of those ashes, to add more coals or when cooking is complete, so as not to get ashes into the food when the lid is removed. A small whisk broom, such as sold for automobile cleanup, is ideal for this purpose. It can also be a handy tool to use in cleaning up the steel cooking table.

WOODEN UTENSILS

One or more long-handled large wooden spoons are essential for Dutch oven cooking. They are soft and will not hurt the patina and they don't burn the mouth when taste-testing. Besides, this was the traditional spoon that was used with the first Dutch ovens. Dutch oven master chef George Prechter would not look like himself if he did not have a wooden spoon in his hand when cooking; it is his trademark. He is well known for using the spoon to adjust a Dutch oven hanging by its bail over an open fire. Also, he frequently taps the lids of Dutch ovens cooking in coals. No one knows what he hears when he does that. And he swears by the wooden spoon when stirring or sampling a dish.

I also like to use a wooden spatula when cleaning my ovens. It will get food out completely without damaging the oven's seasoning.

A good source of high-quality, long-lasting wooden spoons and other wooden utensils is Woodland Interiors of Nampa, Idaho (see sources section for address). I use two of these spoons that are made from maple. They are 14 inches long, which puts the hand farther from the heat, and the handles are beefy, strong enough to stir and lift thick foodstuffs without fear of breaking.

As you get more into Dutch oven cooking you will have your own favorite set of accessories to make your cooking more fun and less work.

Wooden spoons

CARING FOR YOUR WOODEN UTENSILS

- Hand-wash with regular dishwashing liquid, rinse, and dry.

- Often when wood gets wet, it raises the grain. We call these spots "fuzzies," and fuzzies are normal. Lightly sand with 300- or 400-grit sandpaper.

- Rub utensils with mineral oil, beeswax, or another food-safe finish, as needed. Do not use vegetable oil, as it may turn rancid.

- Do not allow your wooden utensil to soak.

Courtesy of Don Bentley, Woodland Interiors.

CHAPTER EIGHT

My first few years of cooking meals in cast iron Dutch ovens were done in wilderness settings using coals from a campfire as a heat source. Then I discovered the fun of cooking for family and friends in the backyard. In this setting it was not possible to have a campfire going from which to get shovels of hot coals to heat my ovens. It was this backyard cooking that introduced me to using charcoal briquets to heat my ovens and I have been hooked ever since.

Charcoal briquets have campfire coals beat in several ways. First, they do not require the work, time, and fuel involved with building a campfire. Using a charcoal chimney starter, charcoal briquets do not take but a few minutes to be ready to place on and under the oven. Quality charcoal briquets burn longer and more evenly than campfire coals. (I have gotten the best results with Kingsford charcoal.) Briquets are easier to place around Dutch ovens, and to move around than loose coals. Under ideal conditions, briquets burn for approximately one hour, campfire coals about half that. Briquets are easy to transport and much easier to clean up than campfire ashes.

ARRANGING BRIQUETS FOR CONTROLLED HEATING

Charcoal briquets are the easiest way to heat Dutch ovens. They give a longer, more steady supply of heat, which aids greatly in controlling temperature.

Arranging charcoal for temperature control is a personal thing with Dutch oven chefs, and the subject of many campfire and backyard debates. Some like to lay their briquets in a checkerboard pattern, both under the oven and on the lid. Others like to place their briquets in a circle under and on top of the oven. Yet others like to use a circle of briquets under the oven and a checkerboard on the lid. I have eaten some great dishes cooked by chefs who used each of these three methods so it depends which method you choose to master. Personally, I like the circle arrangement.

One charcoal briquet pattern that almost all Dutch oven cooks agree on is the pattern used for frying or boiling. Because a lot of heat is required for these two methods of cooking, a full spread of briquets is used under the oven. As the oil or water heats up, the heat can be reduced by removing a few briquets, using tongs.

For most dishes cooked in a Dutch oven, one of five temperatures is called for: 325°, 350°, 375°, 400°, or 425°. (I have found that most of my dishes are cooked at 350° and other Dutch oven cooks tell me they usually cook at 350°.) Obtaining and maintaining these temperatures is a challenge for the Dutch oven cook as wind, air temperature, sun, shade, humidity, ashes, and brand of charcoal can influence the cooking temperature. A strong wind can make the briquets burn extremely hot; accumulation of ashes on the briquets can make them burn cool. Cold outside air can make the pot colder than usual and high temperatures can increase the cooking temperature. High humidity can make briquets burn slow, producing less heat. Whether the cooking is done in the sun or shade can make a difference. Some cooks say it can make a 25° difference in cooking temperature. The point is, you must make adjustments in the number of briquets used, depending upon these local conditions.

Having said that, I will give some commonly accepted guidelines for the arrangement and number of charcoal briquet to use for Dutch oven cooking. I have used these guidelines with satisfaction, and they are the guidelines suggested by Lodge Manufacturing Co. for use with their Dutch ovens. I strongly suggest that you keep a notebook handy when you are cooking under different conditions and keep records of the briquet arrangement and the number of briquets you use for reaching the desired cooking temperatures under the conditions. That is some of the fun and one of the rewards of being a master of Dutch oven cooking.

ESTIMATING TEMPERATURE

The following baking temperature chart will get you started, and with a little experience you will be able to make changes for your local conditions. The number to the right of the oven sizes is the total number of briquets required to reach the temperature. The numbers directly below those are the numbers of top/bottom briquets required to obtain the temperature.

BAKING TEMPERATURE CHART

Oven Size	Desired Temperature				
	325	350	375	400	425
8-inch	15	16	17	18	19
	10/5	11/5	11/6	12/6	13/6
10-inch	19	21	23	25	27
	13/6	14/7	16/7	17/8	19/9
12-inch	23	25	27	29	31
	16/7	17/8	18/9	19/10	21/10
14-inch	30	32	34	36	38
	20/10	21/11	22/12	24/12	25/13
16-inch	34	36	38	40	42
	22/12	24/12	24/13	27/13	28/14

Courtesy of Lodge Manufacturing Co.

Arrange the number of briquets needed by placing them under the oven's bottom in a circular pattern so that they are $1/2$ inch inside the oven's edge. Arrange the briquets on top of the lid in a circle around the edge with one on either side of the handle.

Avoid the temptation to pile all the coals in one bunch, either under the oven or on the lid. When this is done a hot spot is formed, guaranteeing burned food and possibly ruining the oven.

Dutch oven chef George Prechter recommends taking the oven off the coals every 15 minutes and rotating $1/2$ turn. Then lift the lid and rotate it $1/2$ turn in the opposite direction. This helps prevent hot spots from forming.

All of this sounds difficult to learn but it is quite easy and a fun process, especially the testing. I used biscuits as a test food when I was working out the number of briquets and configuration to use on a new 10-inch Dutch oven. I kept a jar of muscadine jam nearby and used it on the test biscuits I didn't burn. Soon I had all my neighbors helping with the test.

I have some friends who don't depend on experience to judge the temperature inside their Dutch ovens. They use a long-stemmed oven thermometer. Anytime they want to know the temperature inside the oven they ease the lid of their oven open, insert the thermometer, and read the temperature. Many do this too often. It allows moisture and heat to escape and there is a greater chance of ashes getting into the food. Also there is a greater chance of getting burned when doing this. You be the judge.

As with any new cooking technique, practice is required to master Dutch oven temperature control, but once you have a system that works, Dutch oven cooking is easy.

CHARCOAL SAFETY

Keep these safety tips in mind as you use charcoal for your Dutch oven cooking:

1. Never burn charcoal inside homes, buildings, tents, vehicles, etc., as odorless toxic fumes may accumulate and cause death.
2. Never use gasoline to light charcoal.
3. Do not add lighter fuel directly to burning or hot charcoal.
4. After cooking, make sure ashes are completely cool before discarding.
5. Cook safely, away from flammable items, overhanging roofs or limbs, and out of the way of playing children or sports activities.

The charcoal briquet fire lets even the newest cook produce meals fit for a king.

CHAPTER NINE

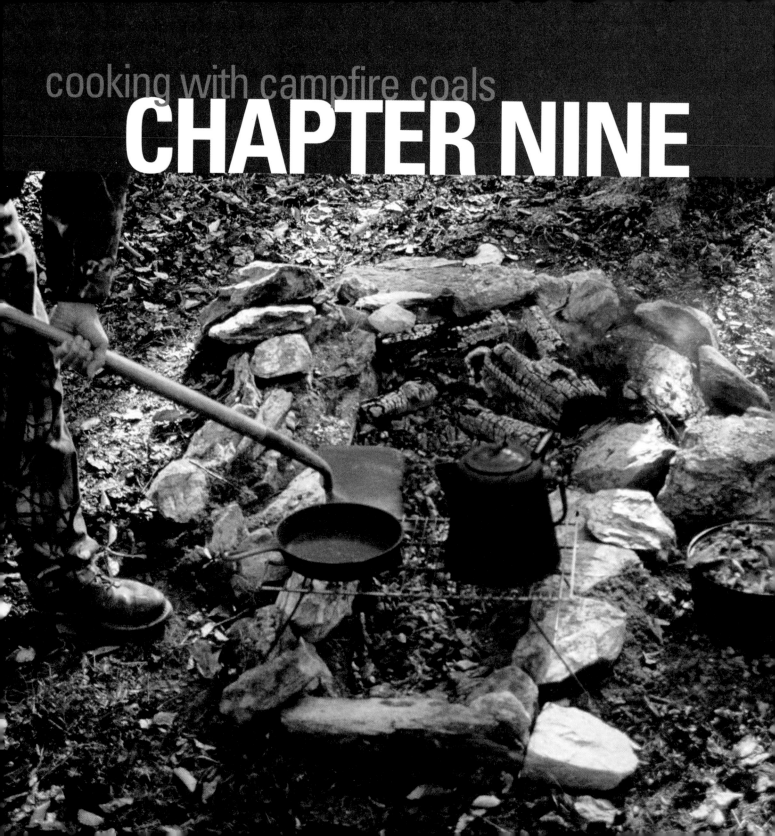

Successfully cooking a Dutch oven meal with coals from a campfire requires more experience than cooking with charcoal briquets. It requires more experience to learn how to judge the amount of coals to place on and under the oven, the heat output from the coals, what coals burn best, and when to replace coals.

When I first started Dutch oven cooking, I thought the more hot coals on the campfire the better, and I burned a lot of food. My scoutmaster said I cremated everything I placed in a Dutch oven. Also, it took me a couple of ruined meals to learn that wood like pine, poplar, and cottonwood don't make good coals for Dutch oven cooking. However, it didn't take me too long to get the feel of campfire cooking and it's been easy ever since.

DESIGN A CAMPFIRE FOR COOKING

The location of your cooking site will have a lot to do with the type of fire you build to heat coals for your Dutch oven cooking. Obviously, in many areas you cannot use an open fire and charcoal briquets will be your only choice. However, you may live in an area where you can have an open fire in your backyard and you may install a commercial fire ring or you may be in a backcountry camp where you can put in a keyhole fire with rocks for days of cooking, or you may be on the move, and a simple fire ring will have to do. The point is there is a campfire design for all situations that will give you a good supply of coals for your Dutch ovens.

COMMERCIAL FIRE RINGS

It is hard to beat a bed of oak or hickory coals.

For those lucky enough to live where it is permissible to have an open fire in their backyard, the commercial fire ring is a safe way to have a fire to produce hot coals for Dutch oven cooking. I have visited many ranches in the West where Dutch oven suppers were the norm, cooked on the patio using an open fire. Many of these ranches have put in an all-steel commercial fire ring. A lot of state and national parks have commercial fire rings that work well for Dutch oven cooking while camping. I have a commercial fire ring at my cabin in Cross Creek Hollow and that is the favorite gathering place for visitors, especially if the Dutch ovens are heating. It has a heavy-duty grill that can be lowered on the fire for frying or boiling in a Dutch oven and when the grill is not needed it is swung back, out of the way, to make shoveling hot coals easy.

When I was looking for my fire ring I found it difficult to find a commercial source and I was lucky to have a friend who had an extra one. Since then I have found several sources. A manufacturer with a good variety of fire rings is Pilot Rock Park Equipment Company. They have fire rings with adjustable cooking grates. The grate tips back out of the way so as not to interfere with getting coals for Dutch ovens, or obstruct the view of people sitting around the campfire during storytelling sessions. Here are some other features of these well-made fire rings:

- Flanged fire ring. The 1-inch top flange is both a safety feature and reinforces the ring against heat warpage.
- Infinite adjustment of cooking surface. You can adjust the grate for various cooking levels.
- Grate tips back for easy fire building. Grate will lift up and out of the ring for fire building and clean-out.
- Three fire barrier heights. Rings are available with 7-inch, 9-inch, or $11\frac{1}{4}$ inch height. Choose the degree of fire barrier you need.
- Unique handle design. The handle design allows the cooking grate to lower inside the ring and keeps the spring grips out of the heat.
- Public-use-type spring grips. The spring grips are coiled from a $\frac{1}{2}$ inch steel flat bar for a safer, cooler handle.
- Fire ring tips back for easy cleaning. The entire ring lifts up on hinges to make clean-out easy.
- Installs without a concrete pad. The fire ring may be installed on the ground or on gravel, eliminating the trouble and expense of a concrete pad.
- Conserves firewood. The cooking grate will lower inside the ring, allowing the user to cook over a low fire.
- Reinforced grate foils vandalism. The structurally reinforced grate design is strong enough to deter vandalism.

The keyhole fire ring gives the cook space to cook and a good supply of hot coals at the same time.

Hot Coals

Main Fire

Pilot Rock makes fire rings in a variety of diameters, ranging from a wood-conserving 28 inches to a group size of 60 inches. Also, they make models that are wheelchair accessible and models that are raised high enough for cooking comfort.

Where were these fire rings when I was looking for mine? If you don't heed all the features of a commercial fire ring, you can make one from a large truck or tractor tire rim by taking a cutting torch and cutting out the middle. However, since the fire ring is an item you will probably buy only once, why not get the commercial model with all the conveniences?

THE KEYHOLE FIRE

Many years ago when I first started going into the backcountry of the Rocky Mountains, I noticed that several of the old outfitters that cooked in Dutch ovens used a campfire design they called a "keyhole" fire. They would pick a safe and logical location for the cooking fire and would take rocks and make an outline that was shaped like a keyhole, round at one end, with a rectangle running from it. The round part would be up to 36 inches in diameter and the rectangular part would be from 12 to 24 inches wide and about 36 inches long. A fire of choice hardwood would be built in the round part and then hot coals would be pulled out into the rectangular part, where it would be easy to get a shovel of coals to put on Dutch ovens without disturbing the main fire. Also, the narrow part of the keyhole would be used to place a grill to set

Cooking with hardwood fueling the Dutch oven dates back to the earliest days of the oven. It still works well today.

Dutch ovens on for stewing or frying. It was a most efficient arrangement for long-term base camp cooking.

COOKING PLATFORM

Regardless of what type campfire you choose to use, you will need a flat, level surface on which to place your hot coals and Dutch ovens. Cold, wet ground will rob the ovens of heat rapidly and leave scorched earth. Many Dutch oven cooks have a heavy-duty, flat piece of metal they use as a cooking platform. Others carry a folding steel cooking table, such as is used with charcoal briquet cooking, for use with campfire coals. I have seen many backcountry cooks place a large flat rock near the campfire for this purpose. I use a flat rock adjacent to the fire ring at my cabin. And, when commercial fire rings are permantely placed, a concrete pad is often poured, specifically to create a safe, level location for Dutch oven cooking.

No matter what type fire ring you use with an open fire you will need a safe, level place in which to cook in Dutch ovens, so give some thought ahead of time as to what it will be. I once spilled a stew in front of a lot of people because I hastily picked a cooking spot near my campfire. The ground gave way under the weight of the full cast iron oven and my guests watched their dinner run out onto the ground. That was many years ago, but I still hear about it today.

CHOICE OF COOKING WOODS

One of the fun debates you will often hear when a group of Dutch oven cooks get together, especially if they are from different parts of the United States, is what type of firewood burns into the best coals to use for Dutch oven cooking. Cowboy cooks from the Southwest will fight for mesquite, Southern cooks will argue for hickory, Northern cooks will brag about oak, and some Midwestern cooks swear by Osage orange.

Several years ago, after writing a magazine article about Dutch oven cooking in *Sports Afield* magazine, I received a call from a new Dutch oven cook from Louisiana. This cook was having trouble getting his dishes done through and through before the outer edges of the food were burned. It was obvious that at some point his oven was getting too hot but it was strange that the food was still raw in the center. At some point I asked him about the wood he was burning for his coals. It was pine. That answered all the questions. The pine was burning hot for a short period of time but burned out quickly. Softwoods are not for Dutch oven cooking, except possibly for kindling to get a hardwood fire going.

What the Dutch oven cook wants is a heat-holding coal that will burn evenly and hot for long periods of time. Consider only proven hardwood fuel wood for making coals for Dutch oven cooking.

Unfortunately, not all hardwoods produce good coals for Dutch oven cooking. Poor choices of hardwoods are poplar, cherry, elm, aspen, birch, gum, cottonwood, and sycamore, to name a few. They will make a good conversation fire, and kindling for starting fires, but will not give hot, long-lasting coals for cooking with Dutch ovens.

In my opinion, give the highest consideration to hickory, oak, mesquite, and hard maple, in that order. I have friends who are master chefs with the Dutch oven who prefer other woods. Medrick Northrop, a great cook in the bush and at home, lives in Alaska. His wood of choice for Dutch oven cooking is pecan, something that is in short supply where he lives. Ken French, known as the "woods wizard" in his home state of Maine, likes walnut. I once watched him make coals for Dutch oven cooking using a supply of "factory reject" rifle stocks. That was some of the most beautiful wood I have ever seen go into a campfire.

Other Dutch oven cooks agree with me about hickory. Arizona Dutch oven expert Stella Hughes, states in her well-known book, *Bacon & Beans,* "I've only had one experience in using hickory wood and it made me a lifetime disciple of this wonderful hardwood. Hickory burns down to a bed of hot coals that keeps an even, generous heat for hours."

Supply can have a lot to do with the wood you choose for your Dutch oven campfire, but given a choice use hickory, oak, mesquite, or hard maple and you will have some good coals for your ovens.

A good supply of hardwood seasoning in a woodshed can give the Dutch oven cook many pleasant meals. When putting up the wood is a good time to invite those you cook for over, to help.

OBTAINING AND STORING HARDWOOD FIREWOOD

If you do a lot of cooking using campfire coals, you will want a supply of firewood.

If you plan on buying firewood, the density of the wood is important because wood is usually bought by volume. The most common unit is the "cord," that is a stack of wood 4 feet wide, 4 feet high, and 8 feet long. Sometimes wood is sold by the truckload, which is a highly variable measure. A rule of thumb is that a half-ton pickup truck is capable of carrying $1/3$ cord of wood. To find out what fraction of a cord you are buying, use this formula: (height of wood) x (width of wood) x (depth of wood) divided by 128. The answer is a fraction of a cord.

The tighter the wood is packed, the more wood for your money. The denser the wood, the fewer trips you will have to make to the woodshed.

With a little effort on your part and a one-time investment in tools, including a chain saw, wedges, bow saw, ax, files, hearing protection, safety glasses, and maul, you can get wood for free or for little cost. If your home or cabin is sitting on wooded acreage, a rule of thumb is that with proper management, one cord of wood can be cut annually for each acre you own. (A local forest ranger or forester can advise you as to how to manage this forest.) This practice will keep your wood supply renewable, as well as beautify your woodlands by removing old and diseased trees.

The USDA Forest Service and some state forests have programs to permit the public to cut firewood of down or dead hardwood trees for little or no cost. Other free or low-cost sources of wood are utility company pruning, pulp and paper companies, sawmills, town dumps, and farmers clearing new ground. Always be sure to secure permission from the proper authorities.

As a side note, I always watch for new house construction when driving around. This is sometimes a good free source of hardwood flooring scraps, which can be split up into Dutch oven fuel. Most builders will be glad for you to haul it away.

If you don't want to cut your own wood, you can usually find a local firewood dealer. When buying wood, be sure it is split and dry (why pay for water?), dense, and tightly packed. If you must buy green wood, buy it in the early spring because it takes months to dry. Be sure to measure your fire ring and have your firewood cut small enough to fit.

Once you have the wood, how do you prepare it for burning? If it is moist, it should be air-dried before use. If the wood's diameter is greater than 8 inches, it should be split and cut small enough lengthwise to fit your fire ring and stack easily in the woodshed. Split wood dries faster than wood that is not split and is easier to stack. Stacking firewood off the ground will permit air to circulate freely in the woodshed and will help prevent ground rot.

Stacking the wood in a sunny location and covering it with clear plastic sheeting can accelerate the drying of wood. It is best to keep the plastic away from the ends of the woodpile to allow good airflow, which speeds the evaporation process.

An interesting and fast method for drying firewood is the use of a solar wood dryer. This easy-to-build device is simply a rack for stacking cut firewood off the ground. The rack is placed in a sunny spot near the cabin and loaded with hardwood. Next, the wood and rack are wrapped in clear plastic, except the ends. A vent opening is designed in the top of the dryer. The sun and air speed up the drying process. This is a good method to dry wood if you are late in the season cutting your firewood.

One way to tell if wood is ready for burning is to weigh a few identified pieces on a bathroom scale. Record the weight and place the identified wood back into the woodpile. Wait a month, and then weigh the wood again. If the wood has lost weight, it is drying.

Another method for determining if wood is ready for burning is to examine the ends of the logs to see if cracks are appearing. Cracks appear only when wood is relatively dry.

Store your supply of firewood in a woodshed to keep it dry and from getting scattered. My woodshed is small but it holds enough wood to keep me in cooking fuel for months. It is made from log siding and measures 8 feet wide by 4 feet deep by 6 feet 6 inches tall. In the front of the shed is a large wooden box that holds split kindling. I built the shed in one day, without help, so a woodshed is not a major project.

Start your hardwood fire early to get a good supply of hot coals before you start cooking.

START THE FIRE EARLY

Good hardwood burns slowly so be sure to start your fire early, before you need to start cooking. I once saw a young inexperienced chuck wagon cook, preparing his first supper on the trail, build a mesquite fire less than 10 minutes before the hungry cowboys came in to eat. It was two hours after they arrived before the meal was ready. That young man learned a very valuable lesson that night and was reminded of it for years.

Start your hardwood fire at least 45 minutes before you need hot coals.

TOOLS FOR CAMPFIRE COOKING

Besides the tools normally needed for Dutch oven cooking, you will need a long-handled shovel for moving coals from the fire to your ovens. As I stated earlier in this book, many cooks drill holes in their shovel to allow ashes and smaller-than-desired coals to fall out.

A whisk broom is handy to use when using campfire coals because you are always dealing with fine ashes and the broom is a good way to keep the oven lid clean when removing it.

Keeping firewood cut in a size to fit your fire ring calls for a sharp hatchet and the knowledge of how to use it properly and safely. Remember, it doesn't take a large fire to produce good coals so keep the fire small with small pieces of wood.

JUDGING COOKING TIME

When cooking with coals from an open campfire it can be difficult to judge cooking times until you have gotten a lot of experience. Neither this, nor any other book, is going to give you guidelines that will get you cooking with campfire coals without some risk of burning food. As with charcoal briquets, campfire coal heating values are determined, in part, by humidity, wind, shade, temperature, etc. Another factor, unlike with charcoal briquets, is the type of wood that is being burned and the amount of coals that is placed on and under the oven: the latter varies greatly from person to person. It is much easier to tell someone how many charcoal briquets to use than it is how many shovelfuls of coals, of an undetermined size, to use.

To remove ashes from the lid when adding new coals or removing lids to serve food, use a whisk broom.

HERE ARE SOME TIPS TO FOLLOW AS YOU GET EXPERIENCE

- When taking coals from the fire to the ovens, try to get coals of the about the same size. Here is where a shovel with holes in it is valuable.

- Resist the temptation to heap hot coals under and over the oven. It takes a lot fewer coals than most people think. You simply need the oven to be hot, not an inferno.

- Place coals in a 2:1 ratio, top to botton. If you place a $1/4$ shovelful of coals under a 10-inch oven, place $1/2$ shovelful on the lid.

- Keep the coals under the bottom in a circle toward the outside of the pot. The coals on the lid should be placed around the inside of the flange. Coals heaped under or on an oven can cause hot spots and unevenly cooked food.

- Resist the temptation to bury the oven in the campfire. I know that sounds unnecessary to say but there are people who do it and wonder why their food is burned beyond recogntion. There is a lot of magic in the black pots but not that much.

- Always, when cooking with campfire coals, turn the oven $1/4$ turn every 15 minutes and the lid $1/4$ turn in the opposite direction. This prevents hot spots and helps keep the cooking temperature even.

- While learning to judge cooking temperature, open the pot every 15 minutes and check the doneness of the food. Keep notes, including the type of wood used and amounts used. In time you will get a feel for cooking time and will be the envy of those who watch you work your magic.

- Be sure to keep an eye on the coals under and over the oven. Coals from a campfire do not burn as long as charcoal briquets and must be replenished regularly.

- Stay with your cooking and keep an eye on the coals under and on your ovens. Many a meal has been ruined by a cook forgetting he was on duty.

- By keeping careful notes and remembering the details of your cooking sessions it will not take you long to get the feel of cooking with campfire coals. One of the best rules to follow is to take a peek at the food as it cooks. These inspections will teach you when to add coals and when to brush a few away.

Resist the temptation to heap coals on and under the oven. That will guarantee burned food.

SAFETY TIPS

Anytime you are cooking around an open fire you must keep the actions and safety of others in mind. Keep children and adults who act like children away from the fire and hot ovens. I once was cooking on a canoe expedition down the Alapaha River in Georgia. Most of the "adventurers" were university professors. I kept the cooking area roped off so that I would have room to cook and wouldn't have anyone stumbling over my ovens. One night I had a math professor slip under the rope and go over to my Dutch ovens. I guess he wanted to see what was on for supper. Without thinking, he picked up a hot oven lid. It was a lesson he will never forget.

Keep hatchets and other sharp tools in a safe place and out of reach of curious hands.

Keep an eye on the wind and keep sparks from flying into dry tinder. Everyone knows that campfires cause many forest and brush fires each year.

Successfully cooking in Dutch ovens fueled with campfire coals is nothing new. Our forefathers did it daily. With a little practice it is easily mastered; you just have to want to and to spend a little time serving your apprenticeship.

Use fire safety and common sense when working with fire. Many grass, brush, and forest fires have been started by campfires.

CHAPTER TEN

A favorite method of Dutch oven cooking in hunting and fishing camps in the northeastern United States and Canada is what is commonly called "bean hole cooking." Dating back to early colonial days, this method of baking in a hole in the ground has survived several hundred years of improvements in stoves, ovens, and baking techniques.

Back before electric and gas stoves were common, miners, logging camp cooks, remote resort lodge cooks, hunting and fishing camp cooks, and homestead cooks did much of their baking in cast iron Dutch ovens in a hole filled with hot coals and covered with dirt. Because beans were the most common dish baked, the term "bean hole cooking" became the name of this technique.

Early American outdoor writer Horace Kephart, in his 1906 bestselling book, *Camping and Woodcraft,* called the bean hole a "bake-hole." He wrote, "Every fixed camp that has no stove should have a bake-hole, if for nothing else than baking beans." He continued,

> The hole can be dug anywhere, but it is best in the side of a bank or knoll, so that an opening can be left in front to rake out of, and for drainage in case of rain. Line it with stones, as they hold heat and keep the sides from crumbling. Have the completed hole a little larger than your baking kettle. Build a hardwood fire in and above the hole and keep it going until the stones or earth is very hot (not less than half an hour). Rake out most of the coals and ashes, put in the bake-pot (Dutch oven), which must have a tight fitting lid, cover with ashes and then with live coals; and, if a long heating is required, keep a small fire going on top. Close the mouth of the oven with a flat rock. This is the way for beans or braising meat.

Lowering the pot in a permanent bean hole.

One of the best testimonials I have ever read about bean hole cooking was written by Oregon writer Ed Park. In the book *Campground Cooking,* Ed tells of cooking a stew in an elk-hunting camp.

4

1. Once the bean hole is hot and full of coals, remove some of the coals and insert the oven.

2. The bean hole is covered with dirt and left for hours as the food slowly cooks.

3. The moment of truth as the meal is uncovered.

4. There is a moment of excitement as all the non-believers gather around the bean hole for the uncovering of dinner.

5. "Dinner from a hole, how cool!!!"

5

"Just before we left for the day's hunt, I shoveled away the burned wood of our campfire and dug an oven-sized hole down in the middle of the deep layers of hot ashes. Then I lowered the Dutch oven into the hole, shoveled more hot coals on top of it and covered the whole works with more coals. Then, I covered all this with warm dirt. That night's dinner was already cooking.

"All day long, while my hunting partner and I let those elk make fools of us, our dinner was slowly cooking. The heavy cast iron Dutch oven, plus the hot coals and earth packed around and over it, held the heat and kept the juices simmering.

"By the time we dragged ourselves out of the canyon we were soaked, hungry, and weary beyond belief. It was my night to cook, and I'm sure that if I'd had to start from scratch right then, I'd not have made it.

"But fortunately I didn't have to begin fresh. Instead I merely took the shovel and scratched carefully around in the snow-dampened earth where we'd had our morning's campfire. Soon I took our small camp broom and brushed away the last of the dirt and burned-out coals that covered the recessed lid of a large cast iron pot and lifted the pot out of the still-warm ashes that encased it. I hauled the pot inside, set it on the dirt floor of our tent, beside our sheepherder's stove, and dinner was ready.

"When I lifted the lid on that pot, the hot-sweet smell of a delicious all-day stew hit us and revived us enough to want more. Silently I spooned out generous helpings for each of us and grinned as my hunting partner dug in with gusto."

BUILD A PERMANENT BEAN HOLE

Each year I hunt and fish with Pam and Ken French from their log cabin camp, named Camp Quitchabitchin, in central Maine. Outside their cabin, down near the lakeshore, Ken has built a permanent bean hole. Miss Pam prepares her tasty dishes that require baking and Ken places the cast iron Dutch oven into the hot coals in the bean hole. The top is placed on the hole and it is covered with dirt. After a day of hunting or fishing we return, uncover the pot or pots, and the evening meal is hot and ready to eat.

Following Ken's instruction, I have built a permanent bean hole at my cabin in Cross Creek

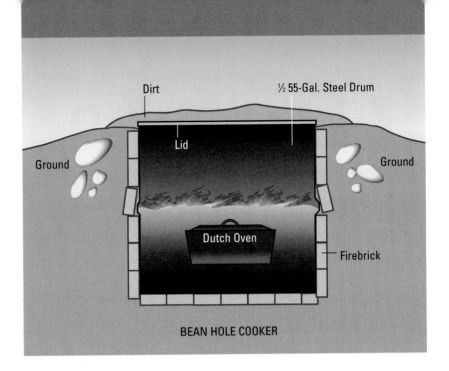

BEAN HOLE COOKER

Hollow in Alabama. Now it is the center of attention anytime I am cooking for a group of guests. Here is how you can build your own permanent bean hole.

Take a clean 55-gallon drum and cut it in half. Save the lid and discard the upper half. In a safe area, outside your cabin or camp, dig a hole a little deeper and wider than the half drum. Line the bottom and sides of the hole with firebricks. Next, drill several small holes in the bottom of the drum to allow water to drain, in the event water should ever get inside. Place about three inches of sand in the bottom of the drum to prevent it from burning out. Put the drum in the firebrick-lined hole and fill in the spaces between the bricks, and between the bricks and drum, with sand. Place the lid on top of the drum and you have a permanent bean hole.

When you want to bake a pot of beans or any other dish, simply build a fire in the bean hole, and when a hot bed of coals is ready, take a shovel and remove half of them from the bean hole. Next, place a cast iron Dutch oven filled with beans into the bed of coals in the bean hole, and put a couple of shovelfuls of hot coals on top of the Dutch oven. Put the cover on top of the drum and cover with dirt or sand. This will keep the temperature even for a long period of time. Go hiking or fishing for the day and return to a hot meal. As with most methods of cooking, it will take a few trials to get the method perfected, but it is fun and, once it is worked out, will become a favorite method of baking in your camp.

One thing I have learned in a lifetime of Dutch oven cooking: there are no experts. Some cooks are beginners, some are average, and some are above average. All, in one form or another, are students. I think that is one of the things most of us like about this wonderful method of cooking: it is education and experience in progress.

When I outlined this book for my publisher, I titled this chapter "Learning to Master the Dutch Oven." As I spent a year working on the project, and testing many recipes under a wide range of conditions, I realized that in writing about all the things covered in the ten previous chapters, I had covered many of the skills and much of the knowledge that go into preparing to take the steps to mastering the art. But you can only go so far with a book. As an example, a book can only tell people so much about temperature control. From there they must learn, based on their local conditions, on their own or cooking with someone who has the skill and is willing to show them firsthand.

So what follows is not a crash course that will make you an instant master of Dutch oven cooking, but hints that will continue to build on the foundation we started in the first ten chapters. These are the hints that will take you to the next level of cooking and will make the actual experience of cooking in a Dutch oven more successful and fun.

Be sure to read carefully and follow recipes to the letter. There are many good recipe books written for Dutch oven cooking.

FOLLOW RECIPES EXACTLY

By taking shortcuts that didn't work, I have learned that a cook should follow recipes exactly, at least the first time. Good recipes result in good food when they are followed to the letter. After you have tried it successfully then you can put your own spin on it.

Dutch ovens hold in more liquids than conventional cooking pots, so adjust liquids accordingly.

One word of caution: I have found a lot of poorly thought out recipes that were supposed to be designed for Dutch oven cooking. Be cautious when trying a new recipe from an unproven source. It may be bad from the start. This can cause a new cook to loose confidence. And don't try out an unproven recipe on the boss to show off your Dutch oven cooking skills. I have a friend who is a wildlife biologist who fell in love with Dutch oven cooking. Soon after learning the basics he went on the web and picked up several recipes. The first time he tried them he invited his in-laws-to-be over for a patio dinner. The dinner was a 100 percent failure. It almost cost him his bride-to-be. Several of us got together the following week to show him what he did wrong. As it turned out he did everything right, but these were recipes that were never going to be "fittin' to eat."

Follow good recipes to the letter and collect good recipes as if they were gold pieces.

LEARN TO ADJUST LIQUIDS

The Dutch oven has a lid on it that fits tightly when cooking and lets little moisture escape. That is great for some dishes and not so great for others. Recipes out of regular cookbooks usually don't take that into account. They are written for standard cookware that lets a good bit of moisture escape. Because of this, any liquids used in cooking, such as water, milk, juice, etc., may make the finished dish too moist. Make notes and adjust the amount of liquid next time.

IF CALLED FOR, PREHEAT THE POT AND LID

When a recipe calls for a preheated oven, take the time to preheat both the pot and lid. Be careful not to overdo it, as you could damage the vessel. I have found that many recipes designed specifically for Dutch ovens start with a cool oven but some, and many regular cookbook recipes, call for a preheated oven.

Cake pans can go a long way toward protecting a Dutch oven from acidic foods.

Also, I have learned that many new cooks burn their bread and pies on the bottom while the top is only half done. By heating the Dutch oven lid, before it is placed on the pot, the heat can be balanced. As more experience is gained, the proper mix of coals from top to bottom will straighten this bottom-burning problem out.

CONSIDER USING CAKE RACKS AND PAN WHEN PRACTICAL

In chapter 7 I discuss the use of a cake rack and heavy-duty aluminum cake pans when cooking certain dishes in a Dutch oven. When I started doing this, it made my cooking go much smoother and oven cleanup is a snap. Almost anything that can be baked can be baked this way. I use them for cooking beans, chili, stew, and dishes that contain a lot of sugar that I think might cause me to have to re-season my Dutch ovens. They do hold less food than an empty oven and you may have to take a recipe to the next-larger-size Dutch oven or refigure the amounts of the recipe ingredients. However, it is a small price to pay for the positive results.

MATCH RECIPES TO THE SIZE OF THE DUTCH OVEN

One of the most common problems some beginning Dutch oven cooks have is matching the oven size that is needed for a recipe. Most recipes designed for Dutch ovens will indicate the oven size needed. However, most of the recipes we use are for kitchen pots of various sizes and must be converted to match a Dutch oven size. Cooking a two-quart banana pudding in a 14-inch oven, using a recipe that calls for a 10-inch oven, will usually quickly result in burned pudding, as it barely covers the bottom of the 8-quart pot. See chapter 4 for average Dutch oven capacities. Take the time to study new recipes and match them to the capacity of your ovens and the pans you use in your ovens. Keep notes. You will be glad you did.

HAVE ENOUGH CHARCOAL OR WOOD ON HAND

There is nothing more frustrating than to be halfway through a cooking session and to run out of fuel or not have hot coals ready to replace burned-down coals. Keep a good supply of charcoal or seasoned hardwood on hand for the meals you have planned. Cold temperatures, wind, clouds, shade, or high humidity can cause a cooking session to use more fuel than expected, so be ready for the unexpected. Having Thanksgiving dinner halfway cooked is a poor time to run out of charcoal.

Also, think ahead. Plan to have enough hot coals to cook your entire meal at constant temperatures. Suddenly realizing that your briquets are about burned out is not the time to start heating up replacements. Your Dutch ovens will start to cool down while you heat up new coals and the meal outcome will be less than desired. Keep hot campfire coals and briquets ready for when you need them.

STAY WITH THE OVEN(S)

I hear from a lot of Dutch oven chefs who complain about burning food after learning the basics of temperature control or say cooking time takes longer than expected. During the conversation you find out that they do not stay with their

Resist the temptation to look in the pot every few minutes.

ovens during cooking or they are so busy talking that they do not watch their pots. Successful Dutch oven chefs enjoy watching their pots and keeping the temperature steady. They rotate their pots and lids regularly. They do not let their coals burn too low or burn too hot. Good Dutch oven cooking requires some attention to the cooking process. To me, this is a relaxing time with my mind on little else but the cooking process.

DON'T SNEAK A PEEK TOO OFTEN

If you want to upset master chef George Prechter, just let him see you frequently lifting the lid of his Dutch ovens to check on the dish. One of the wonderful features of a Dutch oven is that the heavy lid seals in moisture. Every time you lift the lid, moisture escapes and the inside temperature goes down. When you are learning how to cook in a Dutch oven it is necessary to peek every 5 to 10 minutes just to learn temperature control, etc., but once you get the hang of it resist the temptation. Prechter suggests that "dish checks" should not occur more often than every 15 minutes, and the peek should not be longer than 2 or 3 seconds unless stirring is necessary. Many seasoned cooks rarely, if ever, lift the lid on their ovens. That know-how and confidence comes with experience.

BLACK FOOD OR METALLIC TASTE

If the food you are cooking in your Dutch ovens turns black or gets a metallic taste, it tells you that one of two things is wrong. Either your oven has not been seasoned properly or has lost its seasoning, or you are leaving the food in the pot after it has been cooked. Remember, cast iron vessels are not food storage vessels, even for a short period of time. It is best to remove

As soon as food is done, remove it from the hot oven or you can expect over-cooked or soggy food.

food from your oven as soon as it is cooked and place it in a serving dish. Always clean your oven as soon as possible with boiling water and a brush. Rinse and dry thoroughly. Wipe inside and out with a light coat of Crisco. (While the black food that comes from an oven that needs re-seasoning is not pleasant to look at it will not hurt you.) If the problem persists, re-season the oven and lid according to the instructions in chapter 5.

DEALING WITH ACIDIC FOODS

Acidic foods, such as tomatoes and beans, are hard on the seasoning of a Dutch oven and will often require you to re-season your oven. It has been my experience that anytime I cook beans, of any type, in my cast iron ovens they need to be re-seasoned. At first I tried cleaning out the pot immediately after the beans were done but most of the time the pot still needed re-seasoning. For this reason I like to cook beans and any highly acidic foods in heavy-duty aluminum cake pans in the Dutch oven on most occasions. Other than spillover, this protects my ovens and makes cleanup easy. When I do cook highly acidic dishes, such as stews, spaghetti sauce, soups, or chili, without cake pans in my ovens I clean the ovens just as soon as the dish is done. It helps, but I still like to use the cake pans when I can.

I have friends who are very traditional with their Dutch oven cooking and would never use aluminum pans in their ovens but I choose to catch their wrath and use every advantage I can.

DUTCH OVENS COOL SLOWLY

One of the things we like most about cast iron Dutch ovens can come back to bite you in the bottom if you don't watch it. We like the ovens because they hold heat very well. When you cook a dish and remove the oven from the coals, it keeps on cooking for awhile. This can ruin some dishes. I once cooked a beef tenderloin for a group in my 16-inch oven. They were emphatic that they wanted it cooked medium rare. It was, when I removed the oven from the coals. But I got busy with other cooking chores and forgot to remove the tenderloin. When I did remove it, it was well done. The beautiful piece of choice meat had kept cooking in the hot oven.

Any dishes you do not want to keep cooking should be removed from the oven when it is removed from the coals.

USE SEVERAL OVENS AT ONCE

During my early years of Dutch oven cooking I had only one 10-inch oven. It took forever to cook bread, a main dish, and a pie. When I got to one dish, the other was cold. Then I discovered the value of having several Dutch ovens so I could cook an entire meal at the same time. Using stack-cooking, I could cook a meal in the space used by a single oven.

Invest in several ovens and enjoy the pleasure of cooking an entire meal in a short period of time. Also, as more family and friends discover your cooking talent, you will have more dinner guests to feed.

ATTEND DUTCH OVEN COOK-OFFS

One of the best places to learn new cooking techniques, find proven new recipes, and meet fellow Dutch oven cooks is at one of the many, and growing in number, Dutch oven cook-offs held throughout the country. Also, Dutch oven cooking is a major part of chuck wagon and many wild game cook-offs. A day spent talking to, and observing, the cooks who enjoy this activity can give you a wealth of information on the subject. I learned more about what I was doing wrong and the best ways to do it right in one Saturday morning at a Dutch oven cook-off than I would have in a year on my own. And I can say first-hand, you will meet some of the best people to call new friends. If you are serious about Dutch oven cooking this will be one of your best investments of time.

To learn the locations and dates of cook-offs, go to the Web site of the International Dutch Oven Society listed in the sources section.

Join IDOS to expand your knowledge of Dutch oven cooking and enjoy the fellowship of fellow cooks.

JOIN IDOS

The International Dutch Oven Society is an organization you should be a member of if you are reading this book. This organization is the clearinghouse for the dissemination of information, education, and fellowship when it comes to Dutch oven cooking. Their quarterly newsletter, The IDOS *Dutch Oven News*, covers a wide range of interesting subjects. The one I received this week included information on judging a cook-off, new product information, tips on cooking with the little 5-inch oven, recipes, how to build a Dutch oven cooking table, member news, and cooking tips. It's well worth the $15 membership fee. To learn more about this organization, go to their Web site, www.idos.com. There you will also find a wealth of Dutch oven recipes and other worthwhile information.

LEARN FROM YOUR MISTAKES AND HAVE FUN

There aren't many foods that I know of that can't be cooked in a Dutch oven, and taste better for the effort. Anyone can master the skill with a little effort, as Dutch oven cooking is easy once you know the basics. It is an ongoing learning process that is most enjoyable. Don't let learning the basics discourage you. Learn from your mistakes and expand your skills with new and exciting recipes. Most important, have fun as you enjoy some of the best-tasting food in the world.

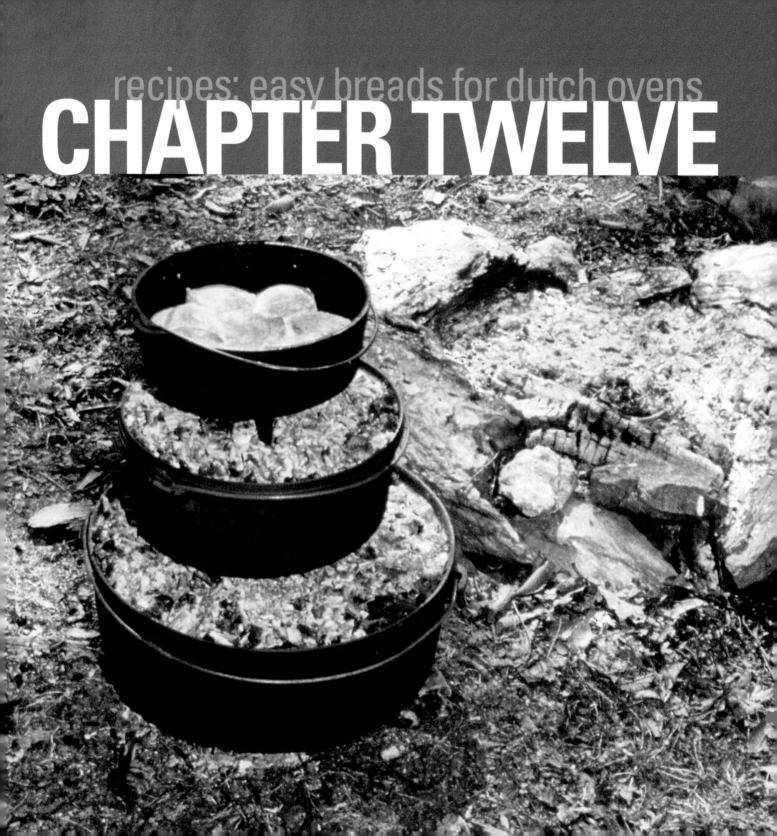

CHAPTER TWELVE

Breads and Dutch ovens go together like a glove and hand. Dutch ovens are easy to bake in and make bread-making a snap, even in the backcountry. It is not only ideal for baking bread you make from scratch but for baking store-bought bread as well.

Because Dutch ovens hold heat so well, don't forget that when baking bread you need to remove the bread as soon as you take the oven from the coals. Failure to do this can result in wet bread, as the water condensation on the lid will drip down on the bread as the oven cools.

An entire book—no, an entire series of books—could be written giving bread recipes that could be baked in the Dutch oven. For this chapter I have selected three basic breads that every Dutch oven cook should know. And because most Dutch oven cooks have an interest in history, two of these recipes have a tie to history.

The first will be bannock. This is an easy bread that was handed down to us through history and is a good bread for the beginning cook.

The second, hoe-cake, is very similar in its historic origin and is simple to cook. The chief difference is that hoe-cake is not baked; it is cooked on the inverted lid of a Dutch oven.

The third is a biscuit recipe that is easy to prepare and is a favorite of cowboys on the ranch where I discovered it.

An entire meal of bread, main dish, side dish, and dessert can be cooked at the same time using stack-cooking.

BANNOCK

Far up in the north country of North America the seventeenth-century French-Canadian voy-agers opened up the wilderness from the Great Lakes to northwest Canada. These great canoeists traveled vast distances on light rations. One of their main staples was bannock, a simple bread of Scottish origin. Bannock has been the bread of the wilderness traveler for cen-turies in the cold north country and is still very popular among those who spend their time in the backcountry.

Bannock is usually cooked in a Dutch oven as a loaf, but you can roll it out and make biscuits. Cowboys on some of the ranches I have visited love bannocks and call them bak-ing powder biscuits.

An interesting side note: this bannock mix can be used for dishes other than bread. I have used it as a base for making pancakes, dumplings, pie crust, batter for fish and as a base for cakes and rolls. The settler or expedition that had a supply of bannock mix could create a vari-ety of dishes.

PORTIONS: 2   **Dutch oven: 10-inch**

INGREDIENTS
1 cup	all-purpose flour
2 level tsp.	double-acting baking powder
½ tsp.	salt
2 tbsp.	powdered skim milk
	water

METHOD
1. Preheat Dutch oven.
2. Sift dry ingredients together; stir in water to make moist but firm dough.
3. Place dough on floured board and knead, handle as little as possible.
4. Place in Dutch oven.
5. Bake at 350°F for 5 minutes.

HOE-CAKE

Hoe-cake has many names. Many know it as pan bread, skillet bread, or corn pone. This bread was first prepared by African American slaves prior to the American Civil War. It is said it was the nearest thing Southern troops, on short rations, had to bread. After the war it was a staple among displaced settlers, and it found its way from there to the western frontier and on to the goldfields of Alaska and the Yukon.

It is simple to make, and those of us who have eaten it for long periods of time like it. It is usually fried on the inverted Dutch oven lid but it can be cooked in the oven as well.

PORTIONS: 2 **Dutch oven: Any size**

INGREDIENTS
1 cup self-rising cornmeal
Dash of salt
1 egg
Enough water or buttermilk to make a paste

METHOD
1. Heat the Dutch oven lid.
2. Add a small amount of cooking oil.
3. When the oil gets hot, pour in the hoe-cake paste made from combining the ingredients above.
4. Let it brown on the bottom before turning.

COWBOY BISCUITS

The world is full of biscuit recipes, some good some not. I have learned, after a career of traveling the world, if you want a good biscuit recipe, go to a working ranch in the American West and get the biscuit recipe that keeps cowboys happy.

I didn't find this recipe at any one particular ranch, I found it being used on several. I thought if it is that good, it is a recipe I need for my collection. I like it because it is simple and you can have hot biscuits quickly.

PORTIONS: 7   **Dutch oven: 12-inch**

INGREDIENTS

1 cup	flour
1½ tsp.	baking powder
1½ tsp.	sugar
⅛ tsp.	salt
½ cup	butter
⅓ cup	milk or buttermilk

METHOD

1. Stir together flour, baking powder, sugar and salt. Cut in butter until mixture resembles coarse crumbs. Make a well in the middle of the mixture and stir in milk.
2. Knead on floured surface a few times. Work dough as little as possible.
3. Roll dough to ½-inch thickness.
4. Cut with a 2-inch cutter.
5. Transfer to aluminum pan in Dutch oven.
6. Bake at 450°F for 10–12 minutes.

COUNTRY DUTCH CORNBREAD

I have always loved cornbread and have made the statement that the only way cornbread isn't good is when it's burned. Well when I first started cooking cornbread in a Dutch oven I burned a lot. Many cornbread recipes are not very forgiving when small mistakes are made in a hot oven. Slowly my family kept working with cornbread recipes until we came up with this one, designed for Dutch oven cooking.

Don't settle for just one cornbread recipe, as it is amazing what you can do with a basic cornbread mix. I have been a judge at the World Championship Cornbread Cook-off and have tasted many outstanding one-pot meals that were started with cornbread. This recipe should get you off to a good start.

PORTIONS: 8   **Dutch oven: 12-inch**

INGREDIENTS

2 cups	Martha White Buttermilk Self-Rising Corn Meal Mix
1⅓ cups	milk
½ cup	oil or melted shortening
1	egg, beaten
Dash of	salt

METHOD
1. Grease a 9-inch round cake pan, heat.
2. Combine all ingredients: mix well.
3. Pour batter into hot greased pan.
4. Bake at 450°F 20–25 minutes or until golden brown.

CHAPTER THIRTEEN

Every Dutch oven cook has a main dish favorite they like to cook in their ovens. I differ only in that I have a lot of favorite main dishes. I think fish baked in Dutch ovens tastes better than fish prepared any other way. Wild game and the black pot seemed to be made for each other. Chicken is great for Dutch oven cooking, as it can be cooked so many good ways and is forgiving of mistakes made by new cooks.

Often, side dishes can be cooked with the main dish in a Dutch oven.

Many of my favorite main dishes are one-pot dishes, great for the owner of just one oven. Other main dishes can be a part of a great feast and cooked with other Dutch oven favorites using the stack-cooking technique. Many cooks use soups, stews, and chili as side dishes but in many of the camps and patios where I cook these delicious dishes are hearty enough to stand alone as a main dish. The following Brunswick stew, Santa Fe Soup, and Zesty Surprise Chili are such dishes.

The game bird hunter will find Big Woods Chicken a favorite way to prepare waterfowl, grouse, pheasant, and other birds of the wild. Non-hunters will find that it will become a popular chicken recipe.

Meat lovers will fall in love with the Longhunter Meatloaf, Tender Roast, and one of my favorite one-pot meals, Pork and White Vegetables. These are easy recipes to follow and almost foolproof in a Dutch oven. If you want to get away from fried fish try the Northrup Halibut Steaks or Cross Creek Salmon. Easy to prepare and no frying.

BRUNSWICK STEW

The Brunswick stew recipe I like is thought to be over two hundred years old. It was found in journals dating back to the 1700s and it has been said that such notables as Patrick Henry and Alexander Hamilton ate this stew at the Cold Spring Club and City Tavern. Dr Creed Haskins cooked this first stew in a Dutch oven in Brunswick, Virginia, and it became traditional at cockfights, rifle matches, and political rallies.

I have slightly changed the original recipe because it called for two gray squirrels cut up into pieces and some of the people I cook for do not like squirrel. Chicken or turkey will do just as well.

PORTIONS: 8   **Dutch oven: 12-inch**

INGREDIENTS

3 cups	shredded turkey
4 cups	water
2	potatoes, cut up
1	onion, cut up
1 can	corn
1 cup	lima beans
1½ tsp.	salt
½ tsp.	pepper
1 can	tomatoes
1 tsp.	sugar
½ cup	butter
½ tsp.	turmeric
½ cup	vinegar
½ tsp.	hot sauce

METHOD

1. Combine turkey, potatoes, onion, corn, lima beans, salt and pepper, and water.
2. Process the above in a food processor until it looks like Brunswick stew.
3. Cook 30 minutes.
4. Add tomatoes, sugar, vinegar, turmeric, and hot sauce.
5. Cook 1½–2 hours on low heat.

SANTA FE SOUP

Here is a good soup for cold days. Also, it makes a one-pot meal when served with Country Dutch Cornbread or hoe-cake.

PORTIONS: 12+   **Dutch oven:** 12 inch-deep

INGREDIENTS

2 lbs.	ground turkey or beef
1	medium onion, diced
2	packages ranch dressing mix
2	packages taco seasoning mix
2 cups	water
16 oz.	kidney beans
16 oz.	pinto beans
16 oz.	black beans
1	frozen bag white shoepeg corn
1 can	RotteL tomatoes

METHOD

1. Brown meat, then add onions, cook 5 more minutes.
2. Add seasoning packages and ranch dressing mix.
3. Add water
4. Add all beans, shoepeg corn, and can of RotteL tomatoes.
5. Place in Dutch oven and simmer 2 hours.

Note: Makes a lot and will keep in the refrigerator for a week or longer. Freezes well, and can be served as soup or topping on chips with salsa and sour cream, depending on how much water you add.

ZESTY SURPRISE CHILI

Thanks to the numerous chili cook-offs held annually around the country there are scores of good chili recipes. This is one a friend gave us and it cooks up good in a Dutch oven.

PORTIONS: 6   **Dutch oven: 12-inch**

INGREDIENTS

1 tbsp.	oil
1 pound	ground meat (surprise yourself) we used nilgai
1	onion, chopped
1	bell pepper, chopped
1	package French's Chili-O seasoning mix
1 can	Del-Monte zesty tomatoes with jalapeños
2 cans	Del Monte diced tomatoes with basil, garlic, and oregano
1 tbsp.	chili powder
2 cans	Bush's chili beans in sauce
1 can	mushrooms (optional, of course)

METHOD
1. Brown ground meat in oil, then drain.
2. Add onion and bell pepper and cook until tender.
3. Add Chili-O mix, can of Del-Monte zesty tomatoes with jalapeños, 2 cans tomatoes with basil, garlic, and oregano, 1 tablespoon chili powder, and mix well.
4. Add 2 cans Bush's chili beans in sauce.
5. Add mushrooms, if desired.
6. Cook at 350°F for 25 minutes, stirring often.
7. Clean the Dutch oven ASAP!

BIG WOODS CHICKEN

Here is a versatile recipe that I first learned how to cook in North Dakota, where the bird was snow goose. Later I tried the recipe in Maine on ruffed grouse. The results were so good I tried it on chicken, something that was in supply year-round, and it turned out extremely well. So if you have game birds, use it for them or you can just run down and buy a chicken. They are all good.

PORTIONS: 4   **Dutch oven: 12-inch**

INGREDIENTS
1	small whole chicken
½ cup	sweet onion, diced
½ cup	red wine
½ cup	cream of mushroom soup
½ cup	cream of onion soup
½ cup	cream of chicken soup
½ cup	sliced mushrooms

METHOD
1. Sauté diced onion in Dutch oven lid.
2. Mix onion, wine, mushroom soup, onion soup, chicken soup, and sliced mushrooms.
3. Place chicken in 9-inch round cake pan, 3-inch deep, and pour mixture over.
4. Place in Dutch oven and cook at 300°F for 1 hour.
5. Serve with rice. Pour the broth over served chicken and rice.

CROSS CREEK BAKED SALMON

I love salmon fishing and salmon eating. Last fall while on New York's famous Salmon River, Ken French shared this recipe with me. The mayo coating forms a crust on the salmon steak, sealing in the juices and flavor. This dish will convert a non–Dutch oven cook into a full devotee.

PORTIONS: 2   **Dutch oven: 10-inch**

INGREDIENTS

1 pound	salmon steak
½ cup	mayonnaise
½ tsp.	Season-All seasoning mix
1 tsp.	Cavenders Greek Seasoning

METHOD

1. Smear layer of mayonnaise on salmon steak.
2. Mix Season-All and Cavenders seasonings and sprinkle on steak.
3. Place cake rack in 9-inch cake pan. Put steak on rack.
4. Place cake pan in 12-inch Dutch oven.
5. Bake at 350°F for 15 minutes.

LONGHUNTER MEATLOAF

This is a simple meatloaf recipe that works well with almost any type of lean ground meat. I prefer venison, elk, caribou, or moose, but beef will do, and when cooked in a loaf pan cleaning up the Dutch oven is quick and easy.

PORTIONS: 4–5   **Dutch oven:** 12-inch

INGREDIENTS

⅔ cup	dry bread crumbs
1 cup	milk
1 pound	ground meat
2	beaten eggs
½ cup	grated onion
1 tsp.	salt
Dash of	pepper
½ tsp.	sage
½ tsp.	thyme
½ tsp.	rosemary

METHOD

1. Soak bread crumbs in milk.
2. Add meat, eggs, onion, and seasonings mix.
3. Form into a loaf and place in non-stick 8½ x 4½ x 2½-inch loaf pan.
4. Spread with catsup or favorite sauce.
5. Place pan in Dutch oven on a cake rake.
6. Bake at 350°F for 45 minutes to 1 hour.

NORTHROP HALIBUT STEAKS

Medrick and Diane Northrop are friends who live in Alaska. Each year they go off shore and get their own halibut steaks. Since Medrick is one of the best Dutch oven cooks I have ever shared a fire with I asked him to give me his best Dutch oven halibut recipe. It's just as good as he said it was.

PORTIONS: 4–5   **Dutch oven: 10-inch**

INGREDIENTS

1½ pounds   halibut steaks, enough to solidly cover the bottom of the Dutch oven or cake pan used in Dutch oven
½ tsp.   rosemary
½ tsp.   garlic salt
½ tsp.   black pepper
½ tsp.   mustard
½ stick   butter
½ cup   milk
½ cup   flour
½ cup   cornmeal
grated parmesan cheese
paprika, and/or chives or chopped green onion tops, thinly sliced onion (enough to cover halibut)

METHOD

1. Grease bottom and sides of pan or Dutch oven to a point above the height of the halibut.
2. Dip halibut in milk, dredge in mixture of equal parts flour and cornmeal with the spices added.
3. Arrange dredged halibut, skin side down, completely covering the bottom of the Dutch oven or cake pan.
4. Cover halibut with thinly sliced onion (optional).
5. Cover halibut with butter cut into pats/pieces.
6. Sprinkle with paprika and/or chives or green onion tops.
7. Cover with approximately 8 oz. grated parmesan cheese.
8. Bake at 350°F for about 30 minutes. Halibut should flake easily. Serve garnished with lemon wedges if desried.

PORK AND WHITE VEGETABLES

This is a dish that came from Germany and serves as a one-pot meal. It may be one of the all-time best Dutch oven recipes.

PORTIONS: 6   **Dutch oven: 12-inch**

INGREDIENTS
3 cups   onions, sliced thick
3 cups   cubed potatoes (1–1½-inch thick)
3 cups   sliced cabbage
1 can   sauerkraut
pork of choice (we used beer-kielbasa):
pork tenderloin, smoked sausage, kielbasa, sauerbraten, etc.

METHOD
1. Layer onions on bottom of Dutch oven.
2. Layer potatoes on top of the onions.
3. Layer sliced cabbage on top of potatoes.
4. Salt and pepper to taste.
5. Layer can of sauerkraut on top of cabbage.
6. Place meat on top.
7. Bake at 375ºF for 35 minutes.

TENDER ROAST

I discovered this recipe when I owned hunting lodges. Often I had clients who complained of venison roast being tough. Using my Dutch ovens I tried different recipes for roast until I found this one. It can take a less-than-tender roast, whether it be venison or beef, and make it tender.

PORTIONS: 4–5   **Dutch oven: 10-inch**

INGREDIENTS

4 pounds	venison or beef roast
	hot water
1 package	Lipton dry onion soup mix
1 tbsp.	Worcestershire sauce

METHOD

1. Place roast in Dutch oven.
2. Make a thick paste from one package of dry onion mix and water.
3. Brush paste over the roast.
4. Sprinkle roast with Worcestershire sauce.
5. Place 1 cup of water in Dutch oven.
6. Cover and bake for two hours at 300°F.
7. Cook approximately 3 hours.

CHAPTER FOURTEEN

Side dishes are as varied as cooks, and what appeals to one group may not to another. The good thing about cooking with Dutch ovens is that whatever the taste of your guests, side dishes can be prepared in the black pot just as easily as in the home oven, whether it is corn on the cob, squash casserole, or asparagus fingers on a bed of wild rice.

What is your favorite side dish? The Dutch oven can do it.

For the purposes of this book, I selected three side dishes that seem to please every guest for whom I cook. These are old recipes that have been proven with time and are just as easy to prepare in a remote mountain camp as on your patio at home.

Macaroni and cheese is a favorite with the younger guests and when you prepare it the way my mother does, it becomes Aneeda's Macaroni & Cheese, and youngsters and adults alike will keep going back for more until it's gone.

High Plains Hominy is a favorite cowboy side dish that city folks take to real fast, especially cheese lovers. The mild chilies add a lot to the dish as well.

Beans are always a favorite side dish, and Miss Pam French, up in Maine, prepares the best. She uses kidney beans, but I have used pinto beans and Jacobs's cattle beans as well. You just need to adjust the cooking time a little for these other beans.

Use these side dishes to get you started but don't be afraid to try your favorite sides using the magic of the black pot.

ANEEDA'S MACARONI & CHEESE

This is a recipe of my mom's that all who have ever eaten her cooking want. She was a school teacher in a remote country school when she met and married my dad, who was a trapper. She has always been a great cook, and I think it was from her that I got my desire to write and cook.

PORTIONS: 4   **Dutch oven: 10-inch**

INGREDIENTS
1 cup	macaroni
2	eggs, beaten
1 cup	milk, or a little more
1 tsp.	salt
	plenty of Velveeta cheese
1 cup	bread crumbs
	pepper to taste

METHOD
1. Cook macaroni in boiling water with ½ teaspoon salt until tender.
2. Beat eggs slightly, add milk and salt.
3. Add egg mixture to this.
4. Pour macaroni in 7" cake pan.
5. Put a lot of sliced cheese on top.
6. Put bread crumbs over this.
7. Dot with margarine.
8. Sprinkle pimento or black pepper on top.
9. Bake at 350°F for about 35 minutes.

HIGH PLAINS HOMINY

This could be classified as a cowboy side dish as I got the recipe from a chuckwagon cook in Texas. A lot of people that do not like hominy say they would not want to try the dish. But once they did they usually came back for seconds.

PORTIONS: 5–6   **Dutch oven: 10-inch**

INGREDIENTS

2 cans	yellow hominy
3 strips	bacon, cooked and broken into pieces
½ cup	chopped onion
5 tbs.	salsa
1 cup	grated cheddar cheese
1 small can	chopped chilies
3	whole chilies

METHOD

1. Mix hominy with onion, salsa, cheese, bacon, and 1 small can chopped chilies.
2. Place ingredients in an aluminum cake pan.
3. Arrange the three whole chilies on top.
4. Place in Dutch oven and bake at 350°F for 20 minutes.

MISS PAM'S BEAN HOLE BEANS

In the chapter of this book on bean hole cooking, I discussed Ken and Pam French's permanent bean hole at their cabin in Maine. Miss Pam is famous for her bean hole beans recipe. She uses aluminum foil to seal in the moisture of the dish and I have found that the double aluminum foil seal does work some magic. Also, you will note that this dish cooks for a long time. Sometimes Ken puts it in the hot bean hole the night before they plan on serving the beans.

PORTIONS: 8   **Dutch oven: 12-inch**

INGREDIENTS

2 pounds	dry red kidney beans
½ pound	bacon, cut into pieces
½ cup	molasses
1½ cups	brown sugar
2	medium onions
2 tsp.	dry mustard
	salt and pepper

METHOD

1. Soak beans in water for approximately 12 hours before putting them in a cast iron Dutch oven. Do not drain beans.
2. Bring beans to a boil and stir in all the above ingredients.
3. Stir well.
4. Cover and seal top of pot with aluminum foil. Leave enough slack for top to fit properly.
5. Place the lid on the foil, then cover tightly with aluminum foil again.
6. Bury in a hot bean hole and cook approximately 15 hours.

CHAPTER FIFTEEN

When it comes to picking favorite dishes cooked in the Dutch oven I would be hard pressed to find something I liked better than desserts prepared in the black pots. It seems the pot adds something to pies, cookies, cakes, and cobblers that you just don't find in other ovens. These desserts seem a little more moist, tastier, and sweeter than the same dishes cooked by other means.

The Dutch oven chef is limited only by his imagination when it comes to desserts.

When cooking desserts in your Dutch oven, it would be wise to use an aluminum cake pan, as discussed in chapter 7, as sugar, fruit juices, and other sweets, if allowed to get on the cast iron will be hard to remove and may require "sweetening up" the pot again.

Back in the days of old cowboys, miners, explorers, and others spending long periods in the backcountry wrote of craving peaches and peach dishes. I have been where they were during my outdoor career and if Dutch ovens were with me so were the ingredients for a Bubbly Peach Cobbler. It is quick and easy to cook and keeps the craving for peaches at bay. I like it when I'm home too.

For a pie that is a little different, try the French Coconut Pie. The first time I cooked this pie at my Cross Creek cabin a teenager visiting ate all but one piece of the pie before his dad realized what was going on. A strong testimony to the dessert.

No battery of recipes would be without an apple pie. Sofee's Apple Pie may be the best apple pie I have ever cooked. It is tasty, easy, and quick. At every camp where I have cooked the pie it has become a camp favorite.

BUBBLY PEACH COBBLER

I was looking for a quick peach cobbler that tasted so good others would think a lot of time and skill went into its making. I discovered this jewel and it serves all of my wishes.

PORTIONS: 6   **Dutch oven: 12-inch**

INGREDIENTS

½	stick butter
4 cups	peaches, peeled and sliced (may use canned)
1 cup	sugar or equivalent
1 cup	flour
1 cup	milk

METHOD

1. Melt butter in bottom of cake pan.
2. Add peaches and sugar.
3. Stir in 1 cup flour and 1 cup milk.
4. Place cake pan in Dutch Oven.
5. Bake at 350°F for 35–40 minutes.

FRENCH COCONUT PIE

Here is one of my all-time favorite Dutch oven desserts. It is always a hit at patio cookouts.

PORTIONS: 8   **Dutch oven: 12-inch**

INGREDIENTS

1	egg
½ cup	sugar
½ cup	melted butter
1 tsp.	lemon juice
½ tsp.	vanilla
½ can	Angel coconut
1	8" pie crust

METHOD

1. Mix all ingredients well, stirring till smooth.
2. Pour into pie crust.
3. Place pie into a 9-inch cake pan and place in the 12-inch Dutch oven.
4. Bake 40 minutes at 350°F.

SOFEE'S APPLE PIE

Here is a family favorite. I think every Dutch oven cook should have at least one apple pie recipe in his battery. It's un-American to be without one.

PORTIONS: 8   **Dutch oven: 12-inch**

INGREDIENTS

2	deep-dish pie crusts, thawed, if frozen
6 cups	sliced Granny Smith apples
1 tbsp.	lemon juice
½ cup	sugar
½ tsp.	ground cinnamon
1 tbsp.	butter

METHOD

1. Combine apples, lemon juice, sugar, butter, and cinnamon in a large pot and cook 10 minutes.
2. Pour into deep-dish pie shell.
3. Cut out apple, stem, and leaf shapes from second crust.
4. Cut strips to form lattice work from second crust.
5. Arrange all cut-outs.
6. Place on a 9-inch cake rack in Dutch oven and bake at 375°F for 35 minutes.

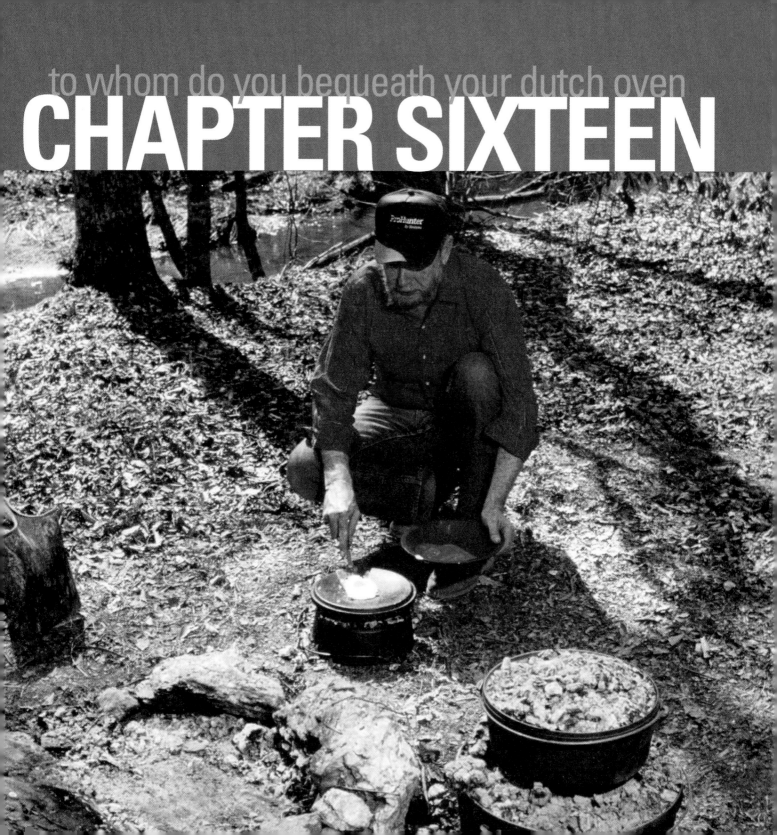

CHAPTER SIXTEEN

By now you can see why people fall in love with their Dutch ovens. After years of tender loving care, hundreds of sumptuous meals, and a learning process that gives a lifetime of fun and fellowship, Dutch ovens have a way of being counted among one's most precious possessions. Earlier in this book we discussed how "iron kitchen furniture" was named in wills of such notables as Mary Washington, mother of George Washington.

Dutch oven cooks usually start out buying one oven, just to give it a try. They had a friend who introduced them to the great-tasting meals these pots produced. Perhaps their interest peaked when the family accidentally attended a cook-off while on vacation. Or they were on a river rafting trip and enjoyed a Dutch oven meal. Whatever the reason, the new cook usually starts out giving it a try with one 10-inch or 12-inch oven.

Most veteran Dutch oven cooks will admit that they almost gave up during the short learning period as they became frustrated with a few small failures. Then one afternoon it all came together and the dish was suddenly perfect. From that point on it became easy, and the food better and better. Now they want two or three ovens, and a cooking table and more accessories. Also, they are getting invitations to come "cook for us." They are hooked, this is a fun hobby, and there is no turning back.

It is easy to get into all aspects of Dutch oven cooking and collecting. I have a friend who is serious about cooking and collecting. Recently, he took a new job that required his family to move across the United States. He told me that it was during the moving process when he got his moving estimate, that he realized how much cast iron he owned. He almost gave his heirs their Dutch ovens early.

My dad's Dutch oven still cooks as it did when he was working alone on cold trap lines. Now I have grown children who speak of their use of the old pot.

Dutch ovens have a way of winning their way into the hearts of anyone who enjoys the savory meals the ovens produce. Because of this they become heirlooms, often giving several generations a taste of their magic.

Many Dutch oven cooks collect not only modern ovens and equipment but also old ovens from the past. It is fun to serve meals from a pot that is over one hundred years old, and even better if you know something about the history of the oven. These are usually in great demand by the family.

Dutch ovens become family heirlooms and I know of some cases where family debates have occurred at a wake as to who will get grandpa's cast iron pot. I have used my dad's old 10-inch Dutch oven for almost fifty years and he used it almost that long before me. It is steeped in family history and has been on many family adventures. Now my children have their eye on it. Who will be the caretaker of the magic pot for the next fifty years?

So give it a lot of thought as you continue the fascinating hobby of Dutch oven cooking. It is a great family activity and chances are good that someday, hopefully many years from now, you will be burdened with the responsibility of whom to bequeath your Dutch oven(s) to. The legend will live on.

Bon Appetit!!!!!

SOURCES

DUTCH OVEN SOURCES

Dutch oven manufacturers

Camp Chef
P.O. Box 4057
Logan, UT 84323
www.campchef.com

GSI Outdoors
1023 S. Pines Rd.
Spokane, WA 99206
www.gsioutdoors.com

Lodge Manufacuring Co.
P.O. Box 380
South Pittsburg, TN 37380
www.lodgemfg.com

MACA Supply Co.
P.O. Box 885
Springville, UT 84663
www.macaovens.com

Charcoal

Kingsford Products Co.
P.O. Box 24305
Oakland, CA 94623
www.kingsford.com

Wooden cooking utensils

Woodland Interiors
Nampa, ID
www.idaholog
    furniture.com

Steel fire rings

Pilot Rock Park
    Equipment
R. J. Mfg. Co.
P.O. Box 946
Cherokee, IA 51012
www.pilotrock.com

Mail order suppliers

Cabela's
1 Cabela Dr.
Sidney, NE 69160
www.cabelas.com

Chuckwagon Supply Co.
1230 Fern St.
Pocatello, ID 83201
www.chuckwagon
    supply.com

Kampers Kettle
2165 Bruneau Dr.
Boise, ID 83709
www.kamperskettle.com

DUTCH OVEN SOCIETY

This is not only a great source for cook-off locations, recipes, and cookbooks, it has hot links to state and regional Dutch oven societies.

International
Dutch Oven Society
41 East 400 North #210
Logan, UT 84321
www.idos.com

INDEX